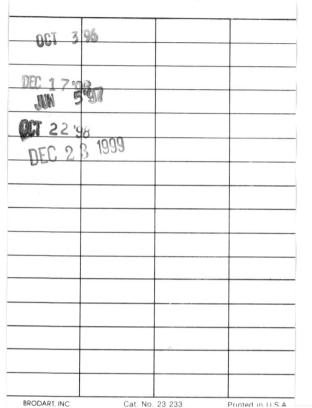

9648

BOOKS BY DAVID DONNELL

POETRY
Poems 1961
The Blue Sky 1977
Dangerous Crossings 1980
Settlements 1983
The Natural History of Water 1986
Water Street Days 1989
China Blues 1992
Dancing in the Dark 1996

FICTION
The Blue Ontario Hemingway Boat Race 1985

NON-FICTION
Hemingway in Toronto: A Post-Modern Tribute 1982

Dancing in the Dark

Poems and Stories

David Donnell

M&S

Canadian Cataloguing in Publication Data

Donnell, David, 1939-
    Dancing in the dark

Poems.
ISBN 0-7710-2833-4

I. Title.

PS8557.O54D3   1996   C811'.54   C96-930054-9
PR9199.3.D555D3   1996

The publishers acknowledge the support of the Canada Council and the Ontario Arts Council for their publishing program.

Typesetting by M&S, Toronto

Printed and bound in Canada
The paper used in this book is acid-free

McClelland & Stewart Inc.
The Canadian Publishers
481 University Avenue
Toronto, Ontario
M5G 2E9

1 2 3 4 5   00 99 98 97 96

For Tom & Sarah & Clarence, Alec Harrison aka "the Slacker," Sandy & her famous Airedale, Martha as always, Wallace & his red Harley & a variety of others too numerous to mention, hello, sunrise.

CONTENTS

"When Janis [Joplin] got it on, she got it on for everybody."

Dave Marsh, *Rolling Stone*, Summer, 1978

"Music is a lot different than television. Music bypasses visual mind discrimination and envelops the inner mind."

Marshall McLuhan, in conversation, 1967

"It's extraordinary what Fugazi can do with a four-sentence song."

David Donnell, September 1995

Saturday we drove across three fields
for an hour, mostly stubble, & came back
onto the road. There was garbage
on the shoulder but it wasn't ours.
                              It was a good day. Eric
is crazy. We broke 2 hampers at the picnic & the girls
left us; they said they would take a bus. Oklahoma,
west Kansas.
            O Wm. Pitt,
                        your Pennsylvania
doesn't rock & roll but it rolls us. Like the old man
at the garage. He was funny. He wanted to know
where Eric got the black eye. Eric has blue eyes.
His wife gave us a piece of raw steak. We ate it at a diner
up the road. Steak & eggs & coffee. The waitress said she'd
already had breakfast, laughed at us. We have jobs waiting for us
in New York. Mine's nothing fancy. I'm going to be a clerk
in a men's store that sells Robert Stock shirts. 3 eggs
& some cayenne pepper. Enough money left over
for apple pie & 2 Stroh's each. A dead dog by the side
of the highway, & endless fields of sweet green peas. I wrote
in my journal, The sun hangs over the fields like a disc
of butter. Pennsylvania is named after William Penn.
The white line keeps pulling like a magnet fixed
to your eyes. The horizon eats you up. Red-headed chickens
when we stop for air. We have cigarettes & gas. I feel excited
about living in New York for a while. I will never become a good writer
like my grandfather because I am too naive. But I am good-looking
& I have guts. I don't think Eric has a job. Plus,
he's crazy. More green peas, more butter that hangs in the blue sky
at mid-day.

I like *The Kingfishers* partly because I love the bird,

                              common

also in western Ontario. But you can look through most of Olson's
poems

        and you won't find a clear description of himself [he
was an impressive looking man & a good agitator], or one of
his friends, or of a black child with an amazing face
modelling a Gap jean jacket in *Vanity Fair*.

Frank Gehry calls his new woven laminated maple strip chairs
after various hockey terms – Hat Trick, Power Play. It's okay,
I think it works.
Some of Feiffer's cartoons are better than most of Duncan's poems,
or Olson's *Maximus*.
I like some of his pamphlets, & I like his occasional use of
numbers.

Although Gloucester is a beautiful idea. A place
where
convention
doesn't pile up and become confusing.

The grackles come out in the early morning and the fishermen
come in before lunch. And those are Atlantic fish, no
fresh water grub.
                    I miss description in Olson
– I miss classic outline
                        and significant detail. But

I like *The Kingfishers*. He builds
a coherent & extrapolative world around his

indigenous
            image. Alludes to some events
in his life
            and has room left
in the poem for a sense
of their strange and almost comic funkiness.

Here I go again – racing forward to catch
the sleek new 6x9 trade paper volume of Wittgenstein.
                                        his
name was Ludwig, you know that much. Nobody really knows
what he was talking about most of the time – it's a long
slow rather dark & anal, if you want to know what I think,
emphasis
            on exactly how do we know (not what/
                                        but this &
or that specific proposition)
                        which we seem to think
casually, I suppose blithely, even the way we might reach
with one summer tanned arm across a dish of orange sherbet
a mulberry smouldering bombe with a hard ferrous & slightly
bitter to my taste Italian biscuit tucked rakishly
into one bulging & voluminous side
                                – for a refill
of the ice-cold Heineken just one more tall ½ full glass
before we proceed to eat the dessert &, of course,
                                        coffee
always, always the rich darkness of different coffee beans
appear like dark oily cherubs in my last dreams
before waking up & rolling over on one long side my body
always seems extremely long at that time of the morning,
6:45 I suppose, 7:15, & cradling you in my arms
your curly dark blond hair & rocking you very gently
O I don't know for about a minute or so I guess. What do I know,
that "I" which at this moment seems to be my shoulders
black Writers&Co sweatshirt crumb of brown rye bread
beside my coffee cup on a page of sprawled blue notes
about a pale young Jew leaning out of a third floor window

in Vienna
　　　　where Mozart ate his kugel where
tribunes of the German Communist party were put to death
in an alleyway
　　　　　　to throw a slice of bread to some brown
white-flecked & slate bluegrey pigeons
　　　　　　　　　　　　it is me, of
course, but I doubt if that is the problem.

Did I really like for real listen for 4½
maybe longer blue jeans checked shirts years
all through high school
                    Malvern Collegiate
when we lived in the east end
& Jarvis Collegiate after we moved to Mount Pleasant
& I had a big third floor bedroom to myself
gabled but huge floor space & windows out on the street
to
    this short, cocky
                    somewhat acid tongued English guy
a ripe huckster
                    plus his borrowed name
Elvis
    Costello?   I guess I did.
That was years ago. Before college. Funny isn't it
how time   •
            & Elvis Costello
& Kate Millett   slip away?   Somehow the story
of Johnny Rotten
                    tearing the Pink Floyd t-shirt,
& writing "SUCKS" across it   in large letters
& then putting it on,
                    seems easier
to identify with than abstract Ping Pong.

$1/2$ of this generation
is going to hell in a basket,
                        or an ABC Dish
or
   an Ottawa flatbed railway car.

                    And $1/2$

of this generation

as long as we're not wiped out by a plague
or personal disaster
                    or a wave of developers

is going to be just fabulous. That's
what I think,
            Tom, okay?

And it's all out there, Dancing in the dark.

Jack Kerouac was a big idol for me when I was 17
in Toronto
& just going into 1st year college –
Trinity for some reason.
I was the odd guy in 1st year. I was fresh from Gravenhurst
up deep in the red & yellow Muskokas;
& by 4th year I was the moody
intellectual
walking around Trinity College on Hoskin Avenue
with my hands in my pockets & my tweed jacket
over my shoulders.

People told me I looked like Jack Kerouac
& I thought that was cool. This was 1984, Kerouac had been dead
for I don't know
a long time, but I had a big b&w picture of him
leaning against a brick wall in New York City smoking a Pall Mall
up on my residence bedroom wall. What else can I say?
I've been reviewing books on & off for 2 years now. Part-time
bartending on weekends in the east end & on Queen Street West.
I've never picked worms with a flashlight at 4 o'clock in the morning.
And I've never been a railway lineman in west Texas.
I've got ideas that are different from the ideas of my generation
but I think it's too soon to release them –
interesting ideas about intellectuals & contemporary music,
new ideas about intellectuals & the labour movement.
So I'm reviewing a few books & taking my time. But as far as
drives go,
what about Miamiiii? Miami in the middle of frozen
New York & Ontario cold weather warnings? What a blast of colour,
forsythia, sweet bougainvillea, the lush blue line of the Florida
coast?

      "Hush now," she says, "I'm going upstairs
to talk to the baby Jesus." The big upstairs swinging
door swings open & shut behind her. A house big enough
to give the 3rd floor over to a kind of retreat.
I lie with my hands behind my head & the sweat
drying slowly invisibly on my thighs, one knee & on my
shoulders. So she's a good-looking young white woman
with a big house but I don't think she's really serious
about this baby Jesus stuff. Maybe,
                        who knows?
Puts her hand between my legs the way you would stroke
some tomatoes or green peppers in a Loblaws
if you weren't too sure of what you were buying
but we're talking about crisp fat fresh radicchio here
not that wilted kind they serve in restaurants
& she says, "Tell me about Mississippi." She's drunk,
I guess. But I tell her a few things I've heard
people say. I don't know anything about that
Mississippi shit. I'm just lying here looking out
at the moon, ½ full, yellow moon behind some clouds,
numbers don't really interest me. I'm on the cusp
of turning 21, now that's important, either this man
I am goes back to school or I don't go back to school.
All I really want is to come & go, leave this city
after the trees, there are trees everywhere here, start
tumbling down & go somewhere & sit tilting the Jim
Beam & the Jack around in my glass watching the Mets
come up from 2nd place, fall weather, an old sweater,
Gooden pumping up the steam; the steam from really good
rich dark coffee beans is different from other kinds
of steam, it's deeper, richer, it draws me in

& I tumble like a butterfly, that's a funny image,
& beat my wings I guess, lift up & away
& watch the game in some neighbourhood bar
where an old woman, Irish maybe, asks me to move
my chair a bit because I've got such a big head. O
yeah, I guess so, but I don't know shit about Mississippi,
& I don't think I like baseball so much
because my father was a black dentist in Boston
or because my mother sings in a choir in Toronto;
it may have something to do with colour,
but I think it's mainly because I don't want to be a
lawyer, and because I don't want to stay in one place
for too long. Mississippi, shit.

All these stories about Jay Mc
                              Inerney
as a youth novelist are a bit exaggerated. McInerney
didn't do very much "youth culture" after he published
Bright Lights,
              Big City. No circuses
                                    or great concerts
or mass gatherings
or serious journalism. No Music, for sure no music.
Life was calm
              & McInerney just hung out in New York
after hours places
              like Nell's
& did what people used to do in diners – drink coffee
& talk about what they used to do back in college
except that in the after hours club version
you're supposed to do a little coke every ½ hour.
                                              O

coke, O coke. I prefer some of the stories
about Truman Capote
                    coming up to New York when he was 19
after writing *Other Voices, Other Rooms* & all the crazy
parties he was involved in after that. I read his short
stories in Grade 13 at Malvern High & I thought,
                                              Wow,
is this guy imaginative. Southern Gothic. Plus,

he had a great admiration for the time signature &
personality of the American sentence.

There was a yellow sky, it was smoky yellow, it was around 6:45 on a June night, and we were sitting, draped over large over-size white-painted wicker furniture, on the long front porch before supper. I was having supper at Susan's, her parents were in New York for the weekend, there was water boiling for spaghetti, we were going to go in soon and make a tossed salad, nothing special, maybe some cracked walnuts and orange sections, and then we were going to go to a film with Ted and Alice.

Something made me think of a Suzanne Vega story, she's a singer, and she does comic monologues when she feels like it, I've seen her on television a couple of times. I said, "Suzanne Vega has a funny story." Susan nods with repressed hilarity, she'd been laughing violently about something else we were talking about, she's wearing a pale mauve shirt, a big loose shirt, one of her father's. She says, "Okay?"

I say, "She claims this is one of her earliest memories, I don't know if that changes the nature of the story or not, gives it a special emphasis. She's about 4½, she's sitting on the floor on the carpet in her parents' living room, Massachusetts or wherever, in front of the television set maybe. Her first boyfriend . . ."

"Just a second," says Susan, leaning forward and almost falling agile athlete over the wide arm of her white-painted wicker chair, "her *first* boyfriend."

I say, "Yeah, her first boyfriend."

"So, how many boyfriends did she have at 4½?"

"I don't know," I say, "this was her first, so it's special, I guess, okay." We've been drinking gin & lemon juice & grapefruit juice & orange juice & cracked ice, I have a little bit left in my tall glass. "Anyway, they're sitting there, and she remembers saying to him, at least she claims she remembers this, and she has every right to claim she remembers this, it's private, sure, but it's her life, right? she says to him very nicely, very seriously, maybe her parents were there, who knows, 'When I grow up, Mark, I'm going to marry you.'"

"His name was Mark?"

"I don't know. I can't remember. We don't know for sure if the story is actually true, or if it's simply one of her stories, I mean, she's a comic, right, or a writer."

"The other kid's name may have been Albert or something and she could have changed it."

"Right, so, that's what she says to him. I like to imagine, she doesn't go into details, that she was wearing one of those really neat little white dresses with a sash, like that photograph of your sister . . ."

"Very proper."

"Yeah."

"They weren't working class?" Susan loves nitty gritties.

"I don't know, she's got a very upper middle class style, I mean, she's preppy, she's got that style."

"Yeah, okay." Susan is sitting up now straddling the wide arm of her wicker chair, she has loose multicoloured Bermudas on and the loose floppy legs of her cotton shorts ride up over her smooth tanned thighs creating an impression not of prurience, she just has white underwear on anyway, I mean it's nothing exotic, but rather an impression of piled-up energy.

"So that's what she says to Mark, if that was his name, if he, Mark, ever existed in actual fact land or not."

"Girls are always saying that," she says, with an odd, wrinkling of the nose, Susan has quite a beautiful nose, not aquiline exactly, not large, a fair-size nose, sort of Roman with a very distinct tip and just a bit delicate around the nostrils. "They usually say it to their fathers. I did. I walked up to my father in the living room, living rooms are the settings for all sorts of stuff, it was one night *after* supper, it was sometime around the time I started school. And I walked right up to him, he was sitting in his favourite armchair in the living room, my mother describes it, and I said, 'Father, when I grow up, I'm going to marry you.' "

"And you've got no memory at this time as to whether you premeditated this dramatic statement, or it just occurred to you, apparently, out of nothing, apropos of something your mother said a few minutes earlier?"

"Oh, nothing, just, you know, one of those 5 million and 1 passing whims that go through your mind if you're a little girl." She leans forward resting her weight on her hands. Susan has beautiful wide strong simple hands, they're not as tanned as her thighs, or her shoulders under the pale mauve man's shirt, probably her father's.

"So what next?" She gives me a big up from under her thick bronzy eyebrows look.

Okay, this is where the anecdote goes Freudian. And it's already turned into a whole conversation, whereas what I thought I was doing was that I was just rattling off a quick photograph, and then we were going to go inside and make a big salad, because Susan loves big salads, even if the leftover balance has to be sealed with Saran Wrap and the bowl put away in the fridge. This has gotten deeper, not difficult or anything, but deeper, sort of like that Sunday afternoon deep old brown hole out in the middle of the Thames River.

I say okay. "So that's what she said, 'When I grow up I'm going to marry you.' And then he stands up, at least I think she says he stood up, I suppose it makes a difference, and he says, 'Well, when I grow up, I'm going to be a fireman, and I'm going to have a big hose, and I'm going to squirt water all over you.' " I'm laughing while I finish the story. I can't help thinking it's funny. It is funny. Most of the stuff that children do is funny. Even though I'm much too young to have children myself, although I suppose if I was careless, I'm not, then I might have. Children. James Purdy has a great book called *Children Is All*, that's what's going through my head at the moment, I'd love to be able to write as well as James Purdy, oh yeah, and other unlikely dreams. I'll probably wind up playing bass fiddle in a dance band.

Susan's hysterical. "Oh yeah," she says between gasps, her violet eyes half-slitted, her mouth coping for air, "that's so true, that's so true it hurts. If you've ever been a young high school girl on a first date, and the boy has a car, and of course you don't, then you know how true that is. The little fats."

She's getting up, I'm getting up, she's clutching her slim flat stomach, also tanned, under the pale mauve man's shirt, still laughing, and tucking in her shirt at the same time.

"Children are so beautiful," I say, guilelessly, "that they can say any-thing."

"Oh sure," Susan says, "and they do, they do."

The story is floating around us like a few distant maple keys in spring floating on a light breeze and drifting down to your front sidewalk or your back porch. "Is she good-looking?" Susan asks, picking up her empty glass and a bowl of salted redskins.

"Who? Suzanne Vega?" She is, she's quite good-looking in a sort of neat snooty way, and I like her haircut.

"Suzanne Nova."

"No," I say, "I think Nova's a corporation. Suzanne Vega, like Vegas without an s."

"Yeah," she says, she's still laughing, "Suzanne Vega without an s, is she good-looking?"

"Yeah, sort of slim and preppy, I guess she's good-looking."

I take a last look at the yellow sky, it's going paler bluey. I'm thinking about boats. I can't help thinking how terrific it would be if we lived clos-er to Lake Huron or down towards Lake Ontario, and we would probably have a share in a boat or a lend of somebody's boat.

"Suzanne Nova," Susan says, "that's funny." She has the empty peanuts bowl, which was, an hour before, full of salted redskins, in one hand, and her empty glass in the other. She gives me a nudge in the ribs with her elbow. "Open the door, Alvin," she says. We close the screen door behind us, and go back into the house to make the big salad before we meet Ted and Alice and go to a film.

Late 60s,
maybe 1970. He appeared
on the lower east-side New York scene –
a young guy
out of acting school and looking for jobs in any play at all.

I read about him in *Vanity Fair*. He just got written up
for a little side bar. I liked
the fact
that he was 6'6", ambitious &
had a small 12x10 room
close to Avenue B,
& that before leaving every morning
he would make his bed & put all his socks
all 6 pair
rolled up, you know,
at the tops, in a row on his bed.
Compulsive, like the history student in Updike's story
Roommates,
but he found work, & guess what,
fortune's play,
he made a # of films – including *The Fly*. Dopey. I liked him
in *The Big Chill*,
where he played the tall vaguely sinister dacron-suited MBA,
It wasn't a great film, post-college sentiment & popcorn,
but he was really good. I think they should make 3 or 4
films in a row like *The Big Chill*, & let Jeff Goldblum
play an MBA,
a mathematics grad-school drop out
& an ex-college basketball forward. He's an intense guy,
& he was good in *The Big Chill*.

We fold up the brown paper bags
& the waxed paper
                        after laying out the food we've bought,
2 steak&kidney pies,
a plate of beefsteak tomatoes,
4 loaves of crusty Calabrese baguette, flour dusted, chewy,
rigatoni with feta & oil & black olives,
cheese,
            put the dogs out in the back yard

& go into the shower together dripping with good intentions.

I am moving the dark blue washcloth dripping with hot
water & soap over one of your hips
                                & then you are
almost reclining on my back,
                        head comfortably
snuggled against my shoulder. I can feel your warmth
more completely than the hot water of the shower. Your
weight seems an afterthought,
                                resting on your perfect
splayed toes,
            down there in the rising water

        When I turn around to face you & we kiss
the dark blue washcloth is I don't know where really.
I seem to rise up & turn around in a sense without
leaving you.
            No, I am still very much here,
feet flat on the bathtub floor,
                        water up to our calves,

your calves are a little fuller than mine,

                         joke, rural,

antecedent, & smoother, no hair,

                            no soft dark fluff.

We kiss, erections aren't a problem

they're a window sill

to lean on.

               You say you are sleepy & would like to make love

& get in between the new cotton sheets & sleep –

you don't want any company.

                       I say "Okay, that's funny,

she's your cousin & her husband's not such a bad guy."

But what I see – kissing your thick dark hair –

isn't any invasion,

                 approx. 7 – 7:30 p.m., & the dogs will be

clamouring to get in the kitchen just to say hello,

but rather that image I've had for several days

of Borges walking through downtown streets in Buenos Aires

showing some visitors around, dark glasses, huge bald

head, gestures, famous buildings.

                    I like the calm way

Borges looks in the image. I thought I was going blind

once, it was a mistake,

                their mistake. I have no

desire to write like Kafka. I like dark blue washcloths,

hounds, & rigatoni.

               I want to see *The Tin Drum*

a third time because I like it as a film. But

I am so in love with the tangible things

of this world   I don't think

you could persuade me to read the novel. The novel

is brilliant but it's too abstract.

"Every woman needs a man
                    sometimes," she says
blithely
as she slips around the dark blue suit who has tried to pat her
on the ass
      & extends one arm, black sweater sleeve rolled up
under white waitress uniform,
              a plate with a wide pork chop, tinned
green peas,
     & mashed potatoes. The potatoes aren't home mash,
she points out good humouredly,
              she doesn't own this place,
a Greek guy does. She has a daughter, Louise, 4½ years old.
"Sometimes,"
I say,   "but not always?"   "Sometimes," she says,
& she goes on to explain that being linked is too complicated
unless you're perfectly matched & even Donald &
Ivana Trump aren't perfectly matched. She's young,
36,
   a very good looking woman with dark hair & just a splash
of entrancing early grey across one side of her forehead.
                      I look
back at that city, Ann Arbor, & I think of her, & think I should have
asked her out, we could have gone to a film, maybe *A Fish
Called Wanda*,
     & she would have been great in bed, I guess, or dancing.
But you know me,
        I like relationships
to end happily
      with both people feeling

there have been no misunderstandings,
                              no distortions
of the kind you find in amateur photography
where sometimes it looks as if Jack is trying to pick
up Carolyn in his arms
                    but it's a blurred image
with a child in the background
& actually he was just leaning over with a hand on her
shoulder to say something to her about the photographer
who used to be his roommate in college.

"What's happening, momma?"
                                        he says jovially
as he comes through the door,
                        not famous as jazz musicians go
but famous enough, about medium height,
                                        close cut hair,
a yellow & brown check sports jacket
but it looks good on him. There are about 2 cars parked
up over the curb outside, we're having dinner,
& I realize there are certain idioms that are exclusive,
that is,
            they go with a specific vocation [software writer,
hardware installation team supervisor, etc.] or colour,

colour at least in the broad American sense
in which the landscape of America is so large it contains
every colour
                from cactus flower yellow to pale blue Massachusetts
fence in a small town back yard.
                                    And just for a split nano
second I envy him & resent the fact that I can't use any idiom
I happen to feel like using. Well, sure, I can,
use any idiom I feel like, using. And then I reach over to
shake his hand
                & I say, "Good to meet you, Coy, I love your work."
And I do, he's a great piano player, and every idiom is like a
bass motif that you can play if you like, as long as it works.

So,
      this guy Harold,
            26, a bit of a nebbish
out of college, NYU,
          a big yellow bow-tie, etc.
shows up at the Blue Note when it was on 52nd street in the 1940s,
& dig this,
      he was something of a writer when he was at college,
NYU
   & this is the late 1940s,
            1946 to be preeeee/cise,
but like hey, a reeeeeally bad poet,
            no intellect
& NO sense of hoooomour.
             And there he is leaning on the bar
& waddda ya think he sees? Some guy
             called Wallace Stevens
is up on stage reading a poem about Kentucky & grackles
& talking about Hart Crane
& a young black dude is playing bass oboe behind him.
"Wow,
    fuck," says Harold the nebbish
just out of college, NYU, big yellow bow-tie, etc.
"so the text doesn't mean diddle-fuck, I'm saved, I'm alive,
I can pretend I'm a writer like Thos. Wolfe or somebody.
So,
   where do I meet somebody who plays a mean bass oboe
or a violin,
      or maybe a French horn would be good
for an afternoon reading in Central Park?"

I'm over at Jack Forbes' 2½ storey 6' skylights
on the west side
                    house on Chestnut Park Road in northeast
Rosedale. Jack's out,
his wife Carol is home
                    & there's a copy of the *New Yorker*
with a fairly good R. Crumb cover in about 9 different colours
lying on the coffee table. She says she thinks the *New Yorker*
is still good,
                    just because it gives you the taste of New York.
Atmosphere is what she means, I guess, hints & flash cards.

But I'm not sure if a taste is much good when you want supper,
you know,
                    when you want a couple of gin&tonics with lime & ice first,
& then a bowl of black bean soup
                    followed by a plate of fettuccine
with those small Italian sausages & 1 or 2 cold Heinekens
to wash it down. You know
                    what I mean? More walk arounds
in different areas of New York, more input from young artists,
put Tom Stoppard on the cover and a 4-page essay on Bill Clinton;
but of course they haven't done this & now it's just another
version of the *Atlantic* or *Harper's* –
but they've got an R. Crumb cover & Richard Avedon photos of Dinkins
& colourful New York lead-in pages with a nice magenta
poster of Eartha Kitt.

He calls his sister Bones,
                              because she's 5'10½"
& as slim as a bright green stalk of west Florida asparagus. "Hey,
Bones," he says, or
                    "Turn down the football game, Bones, I'm on
the phone
in the kitchen." And she takes it gracefully. She's sprawled
on the living room 4-part couch,
                                  watching,
long legs in snug new Levi's, feet bright in orange & yellow socks,
skimpy t-shirt just a piece of cotton.
                                        The B.C. Lions destroy
Baltimore. She has short curly dark honey blond hair, she
is in 4th year English Lang
                            & Lit. It's 9:00 p.m., darkness
has settled
over the huge city of Toronto, the wind outside is about 50 mph,
the huge lake at the south end of the city must have 10' waves,
nothing like a tsunami but big,
                                & the television set full of colour
shows the B.C. fans in t-shirts the cheerleaders in short skirts
& Austin has just thrown a big long one for about 65 yards. "Pizza"
he says, "B.C. wins, I pay." He hates football, loves computers
& basketball, is working now, good quality dark green corduroys,
makes a big paycheque for 25. "Anchovies," she says; "No," he says;
"You're cruel," she says, & Passaglia kicks the big one
that wins the game, & the B.C. crowd goes wild.

Night in the city
                    splash of burnt mauve
across the end of an alleyway,
                    must be old paint. Slacker

aka Alec
          Harrison & Tom, walking home from the BamBoo Club
up Beverley & over to Huron, named after the Hurons
who lived in Ontario
                    before there was a Ford Motor Company
of the World
          or those old General Electric red brick buildings
along Dupont west of Yonge Street. "What do you think, Tom,"
Alec says, "what
                    do you think of the city?" "Great, man,
just
fucking great." Tom is drunk, stumbling slightly, steel rims
in his jacket pocket
                    he has a long pink t-shirt on
& the t-shirt says N I R V A N A. "So,"
says Alec, aka Slacker, "what do you think of the scene,
                                        the cool
Lauras & Harolds,
          at the Left Bank & the BamBoo?"
"Hey," says Tom, "Slackers with expense accounts
& cordless telephones, fettuccine with eggplant & Italian sausages."
"No,
     no," says Slacker, aka Alec Harrison, "Slackers with nose rings
& exposed underwear
defying gravity." "Yeah," says Tom, "gravity, man, gravity."

Tom & Slacker live together for about 3 months
– it's a 2nd floor over an appliance store
on Broadview
in the east end. 2 guys, both in their 20s,

they get along very well. Tom's philosophy books are piled up
beside his armchair
in the living room,
which has a view of Broadview. Slacker's tapes are piled up
on top of an orange crate bookcase
at the far end of the room. They have separate beds,
in case you were curious,
1 bedroom & 2 beds. They both shower quickly,
Slacker is neat,
they split laundry duty on a weekly basis,
& their eating habits are fairly similar –
hamburgers,
pizza, take out hot&sour soup from Bo Bo's,
Chef Boyardee spaghetti. Slacker wears work pants,
Tom wears corduroys. They argue about music, that is
Slacker
says, "Okay, the Mahler stuff, I don't disagree
with it. But you've got really bad taste in rock lyrics.
Like all intellectuals, you don't get the point. You like
Bruce Springsteen and Patti Smith too much. Post punk new
wave isn't supposed to make semantic sense. It's free form because
free form makes me relaxed,
and it *has to have* irrational bursts

of senseless bass violence
because I've got aggressive circuitry in my left occipital zone.

I agree I listen to too much of it,

                              Okay, Tom,

Okay?"

We were sitting up on the roof a few nights ago, it was about 2 o'clock in the morning, it was hot, we were eating crackers and some pale yellow Kraft cheese from the 7-11 and demolishing 2 or 3 litres of cheap white Spanish wine. I guess there were about 7 or 8 of us. It was late and it was casual. You could hear faint traffic sounds coming down from Queen Street in the dark air.

We're all musicians except for Karen, Scott's girlfriend, who was sitting with her legs stretched out in a long line and her back against the low brick & tar wall of the roof with her beautiful short-cropped pale brown head asleep against Scott's shoulder. These guys are all about my age, I'm 23, and mostly from Toronto, although I'm from Manitoba, Dick is from New York, and Paul used to play with a couple of groups after school in Halifax. Halifax is in Nova Scotia.

Ned was talking about music, and how important it is, guys playing in bands, changing the world or something, and how we all want to be famous, but we're only going to be famous for about 15 minutes.

I didn't say anything. It was late, it had been a long day, the air was just starting to get lovely and cool. And I'm usually a fairly quiet guy. I hold myself in. I'm a hot bassist, that's what I play, that's what I do in life, dude, I play bass, people have been saying I'm pretty hot; but if you come from a town south of Great Slave Lake, just a bit north of the Dakota border, and you're in a city like Toronto, with all these different groups, or New York, then I think it's sort of dumb to come on mouthy whenever you get the chance. I'd rather be just easy-going reflexive, take my time and give myself time to think about some of the ideas that people like Ned rap down. It always comes together for me a few days or a few weeks later, and I'll say, O yeah, I see what I think about that. Whether it's music, or maybe art, or something to do with economics, how the Japanese are buying into the entertainment industry or something like that, or, perhaps, something to do with fame. Like, what is it, what does it mean?

I'm 23. I haven't lived in Toronto for very long. Well, about 11 months.

Manitoba is sort of classical. Toronto is an incredible hodgepodge. I think a lot of that goes into people's music.

Anyway I'm not a punk. Not since I was about 12. Before I began playing and took up bass in high school. None of these people sitting around eating fake Kraft yellow cheese and listening to Ned trying to act like a talk show host or a media guru or something like that are punks either. I don't look like that or dress like that. As for the playing, well, that's different. I like songs that seem to be about an issue of some kind. I like people like this guy Adrian who has started hanging around a lot who can write songs that are really sort of "in your face." That's a term, it just means, direct, challenging. But I'm more interested in the bass lines of a song, and how the bass lines can take over the song and make it into something really incredible. What went wrong with Johnny Rotten? He didn't understand the idea that bass is more important than lead, that's what went wrong, so all his stuff with PiL sounds incomplete and sort of tinny, like not quite whatever it's supposed to be.

There's a girl here with the same name I have, almost. Her name's Samantha. She's sitting on a little flat car cushion of some kind, in the circle, across from Karen, and she has one of those really light frilly around the shoulders pink & print summer dresses on. Sounds frilly but she seems to be a really ballsy girl, super pretty, with a ton of honey blond hair. She's talking to Paul about some of the young kids who come into the store, a trendy brass fittings place just off Queen Street West, where she works, and she says, "They're just a bunch of high school kids who like Duran Duran." and Paul laughs. That's how people communicate. We'd be lost if we didn't have these 1000s of different groups to use as designations for what we're talking about. A teacher I had in Tremlo, Grade 12, I think, said it was sort of like the Greeks and Greek mythology. The Greeks had a lot of Goddesses like Diana and Hecate.

I'd like to say something to her, start a little rub of some kind, but I'm too tired. Now she's talking about buses plunging off cliffs in Peru. Lebanese rebels blowing up embassies with car bombs. Somebody says something about children being given heart transplants in Utah. This is wild, isn't it, or maybe it's what you talk about all the time over 6 o'clock dinner.

"Books never stay around," Ned says to somebody who has said something about books. It's dark and I'm lying almost flat on my back with my head resting against an old pillow with some sort of cover around it.

Samantha says, "The Great Books stay around." She must be a reader, maybe she's a student, and she just works part time at the little brass fittings store. That sure is an attractive pink dress, with big splashes of green print you can hardly see, even with a moon, up here on the roof, in the dark. But, I think to myself, we're not in the dark. We're in the light, or maybe we *are* the light. What the fuck. Who can say we're not?

I'm going out with a girl right now, Alice, who works in the UofT library, knits macramé, that's something she does, okay? and smokes some very good dope. She has lovely breasts. We take showers together. She seems to like Mozart a great deal, but we get along and she seems to like the guys I hang around with fairly well.

Punk is very kicksy. Very trendy. But it's also very principled. Punk concentrates almost entirely on immediate attitudes. Punk songs are deemed successful if they do a good job of simply making a hook – take a single word, sometimes a phrase, and then play it with this catchy sound mix that sort of completes a basic take on that one attitude. I didn't pay a lot of attention to the philosophy courses at UofM when I went there, but I think what I'm describing here is a fairly complete aesthetic. It's complete, but the bass is all-important, that's where I come in, and I'm hot right now, 2 or 3 groups have come on to me in the last month, I'm a bit of a star. And according to Ned, or what he was talking about 5 minutes ago, of course, and this is an interesting comment on people who say, O so&so is just going to be famous for 15 minutes, that, itself, was 5 minutes ago, and his remarks have sort of passed, like cigarette smoke, gone up in air, they're drifting off into the dark night air above Richmond south of Queen.

What makes Alice so attractive to me, I think, the librarian with the wonderful breasts, is that she's not a punk, she's this beautiful, easy-going, everything more or less in order . . . librarian. Which is comfortable. We don't have any problems.

"Well, it's like dope," Ned says, "what does dope do for you? It makes you feel relaxed." I think every social area has guys like Ned, who have to define and over-define the different things that are going on, without necessarily really understanding them very well. But sure, that's what dope does, generally, for most people.

But what the bass does is sort of similar and almost opposite. Bass opens up the whole body to a simple idea – an idea which the singer has to be in command of, and which he, or she, I'm crazy about this girl Mary Margaret O'Hara, for example, is responsible for getting across. But when a good bass does that – it has to be a hell of a lot more than just an extension of percussion, it has to be playing some wild and complex lead notes down at the level of percussive rhythm, and sort of flirting with the backbeat, or maybe, in some cases, doing away with it altogether, but anyway, all at the same time.

You need to know something about language, melodies, engineering terms, different kinds of sounds.

Maybe we will be famous for 15 minutes. Or maybe we've already changed a number of attitudes – to things like body language, or dope, or what certain attitudes mean. A lot of kids are just going to wind up on the street, you know, wearing those silly red bandannas over their heads, or funny haircuts, the whole head cropped grey & stubbly and just a patch, like a big pool of ink, like a scalp, floating on top of their dome. Sure, but that happens with every social change. I think Ned's trying to talk about Thailand now. He probably doesn't even know where it is. I think it's next door to Vietnam or Cambodia. I'm just going to close my eyes and drift for half an hour, nod off, half-closed eyes, watching this beautiful girl in the pink&greensplash print dress moving her legs back and forth like a stationary dancer in the dark, car sounds, Paul talking about raspberry pie with ice cream, sounds good. I'm not going to wind up on any street corner, or hanging out at some dick bar or coffeehouse; I'm going to get behind the best singers that come along, the best singers, with the best songs, I'm going to put down bass lines that they can move around, dance, sing, for hours.

I have a copy of Dany Laferrière's *An Aroma of Coffee*
sitting at the far end of the long table
                              where I sit & work
in the morning. This is a clear & blue morning
about -10° with some random patches of white snow. The kind
of January day I like although I'd probably rather be in St. Kitts
or the rural market-gardening west side of Florida. I'm trying to think
about what dark pigmentation has to do with anything
except that it's a colour. Okay, different people have curly black
hair,
        or blue eyes, or blond hair, or grey eyes, or hazel eyes. And
I think, it's simply a tradition of colour *coding* – practised by various
dark pigmentation & lightly coloured Americans. Charlie
Parker was a genius, period, I don't see him as a *black* musician.
Mike Tyson is a boxer, that's what he does. Nina Simone is a singer.
I'm not crazy about Billie Holiday at times because
she doesn't state the pain & then rise above the pain. Laferrière's
book is an extraordinary novel because it's so clear
& so evocative. You can just read it one sentence at a time
& it's simple, but it adds up to a complex image
& it's perfect. It's a book about a place, Haiti, in this case,
where he was born   before he came to Montreal & then to Miami,
& also
        a period in your life when sometimes you're a child
& sometimes you're letting go of childhood – & then of course
you'll probably have to send a postcard from a different city,
Miami, & you'll say things are good here, & you'll probably say
it in French, always in large distinctive writing,
not black but simply
the writing of a person   with a great visual sense of detail

& a very clear mind.

I think Dany Laferrière
& Wynton Marsalis are both dark pigmentation Americans.
I would describe myself as a lightly coloured American. Not
as a "white."

Actually Dany's postcard arrived in dark blue
Pentel,
blue is a contemplative colour
& it's his story as he sees it now from Miami.

I call the largest of the 2 Great Danes
Alice,
     he's the largest of the 2, & 3 months older. The female
is William,
          because Gertrude Stein loved William James,
the author of *Pragmatism*,
for his quirky and generally exact intelligence.
                              This is
Laura speaking, she
               says, "I think you like Alice because he's
got such a big schlong,"
                    & she laughs, she's standing here
on the front lawn of her parents' summer house in Uxbridge
wearing a sleeveless wide-vent pale lemon yellow blouse
& loose floppy plaid shorts. She has great legs, long & tan,
but you can't see much above her knees
one of which has a grass stain. I'm leaning over Alice
who has come out to meet me with my hands flat on his shoulders
his big head is almost up to my waist
he's huge and he's 3 years old & still acts like a puppy.
There is nothing sexually weird going on here. All the tragedy
in the world is in New York City. They have a monopoly. This is
like west Massachusetts. Sort of, as the garage mechanic says.
The ½ ton pick-up has at least 80 or 90,000 kilometres left.
Kilometres are Canadian miles. I laugh. We have tuna salad for supper
& whole wheat bread.

"What is significant
about the Contemporary Novel?"
Those moments when we see
one of the characters we met in Chapter 1 do something
unusual,
something that moves the character,
let's call him Tad,
& the novel as well for a few pages
out of the general coherent OldAmericanNovel sludge
of Dick worrying about his marriage
& Caroline inviting people
for dinner
& Hal & Mark travelling to Thailand
[which by itself sounds interesting, perhaps]
into
a specific module of experience we can identify with
as something interesting – Tom & the Bouncer at the Edgewater
Hotel
down by west Sunnyside; Whitney picking up the cowboy
at Pearson Int'l Airport as she comes back from Germany;
Carol destroying Frank's total Mac filing system; Carter
shooting his neighbour's pitbull right through the head
with one clean shot. Sort of like *Hamlet*, sort of like *Port
of Saints*, sort of like *The Beggar's Opera*. The rest is boring.

Novels like *The Great Gatsby*
cf
the life & times of Jay Gatsby
in the context of American capitalism
do give you
a clear feeling of participating in a sincere & descriptive
essay about financial blood stains on the white table
cloth of our national lives;
but all these chic slim novels
set over a weekend in Mexico
or 2 or 3 months
in the south of France
or some indeterminate period of time
in Berlin –
Berlin without, as far as we can see,
the almost dizzying hugeness, conflagration of odd scraps
of diverse dispossessed humanity,
the darkness of Berlin
at night, the other-planet sense of far off lights red yellow
white blue winking at you from different boundary lines. Other
questions come up – is Sarah really a woman just because
the novel is written by a woman? Is her husband Gerald an engineer
or was this just a fancy on the part of the novelist. What most
of these novelists are doing is merely suggestive. The blond
husband with a large moustache
who is supposed to be an engineer sounds like a carpenter
or an office manager.
The landscape of Mexico never appears.

When he was 12, Tomaszo Garrone, Tom, The Stick, because he is tall and thin with a big sad irregular face that breaks into unexpected smiles at the drop of a hat, had a bizarre encounter. It wasn't his first bizarre incident, but perhaps the first involving extreme heights. The incident will mark him in various ways for the next 20 years of his life. Although later on, age 27, in Texas, where he has landed, his sexy, angsty friend Whitney, genus female, species angel, will suggest that there may be some relevance to this early experience; and Tom will get indignant, red-faced even, and deny her assertion outright. Almost as if she had criticized his intelligence, or suggested that he only loved her because she kept rejecting him, or she had said that he wanted sex with his mother. Surely for an Italian boy, or an American boy, probably the worst of calamitous venial sins.

Toronto is different from the rest of Canada, something like a northern Chicago without as many steel mills. Tom is living on Grace Street with his parents in the large sprawling Italian sector of Toronto, and attending Michael Of All Angels public school on Dovercourt Road. He is fluent in English, speaking it from childhood although he was not born in Canada, he came here, at 6 months, not in his mother's but in his father's, Giuseppe's, arms; Tom even speaks a little Latin, tall for his age, which seems oddly indeterminate, freckles, dark, sort of handsome for an awkward boy, with a very determined chin, a *polpaccio*, a calf, pale. But the calf loves Toronto more than Orillia, which was Stephen Leacock's summer home; Toronto is larger, bustling, sprawling, full of new sights, smells, people, streetcars, things to look at.

(He doesn't know the city very well yet, but is hotly, moistly interested in everything about Toronto. They, the Garrones, including Tom's sister, Fran, and his younger brother Paolo, have moved from Orillia, where Tom's father was employed as a day labourer in the Caterpillar factory. Tom hasn't really settled in yet. It takes time to settle into a new school, and time is an infinite, and infinitely fine, white elastic band that stretches somehow in the upper strata of blue air between southern Calabria, where a man will take a loaf of bread in one hand and a knife in the other and sit down to have lunch. Tom has 2 or 3 friends at school, a mixed school, some Italian, no one from his region, several Romans as a matter of fact, a beautiful angelic girl from Turin, a lot of Anglos, all indiscriminately dismissed as Anglos, some Polish kids, one Jewish boy who wears a yarmulka to school on Fridays, which is their Sabbath, apparently. There are 2 Chinese boys, brothers, the older one is George, the younger is also called Tom.)

So anyway, the encounter, which will eventually be reflected in Tom's life after college, and in various songs he will write during that intense concentrated period at age 27 when he does pretty well almost nothing except write songs.

Tom is on his way to Saturday morning basketball practice, as per usual. It is October, Indian summer month in southern Ontario, when everything is crisp and pleasant and sunny; and it is still 1972, it will be for at least another 6 weeks. Not the year of the first dizzying dizzy dean erections, that was last year, before March, sometime before spring, when the sap began bursting in the Orillia maple and elm and evergreen trees; Nixon and America are still in Vietnam. American television and the CBC are still observing the landscape, usually showing rice paddies, not napalm.

Tom is on his way to Saturday morning basketball practice at a local church, big for his age but fairly innocent, *innocente*, and he runs into 2 new school acquaintances, Spud Arnetson and Billy Flaherty. They talk bicycles and fart around and jam a bit at the corner of Ossington and Bloor; and Tom winds up being talked into a quick subway visit to the much-publicized CN Tower south of downtown on the Lakeshore.

Spud Arnetson and Billy Flaherty, an Irish kid, take Tom up to the top level of the newly built CN Tower south of King Street and, as a joke, a yoick, a kibitz, harmless, nothing serious, 465' above street level, despite the fact that he is tall for his age but also skinny and ambivalently bold and shy, they hang him out by his heels over the 5½' glass-bricked – from Pilkington & Co., world famous for the best glass bricks in the world – guard rail, holding him there above the city, his huge dark grey eyes full of traffic, streets, and a confused image of the infinite blue lake, for a full

5 minutes until a redhaired young 25-year-old security kid originally from St. John's, Nfld., where, listen you miserable fuckers in Mississippi, the most experienced serious drinkers and eschatologically good-hearted bar-room brawlers in North America drift around a famous street – it is called Duck Street and has 350 licensed bars and emporia plus a fantastic view of St. John's Harbour where nobody makes any money, except for the Lundrigans – intervened and stopped them. They would have stopped anyway. Spud and Billy weren't crazy, probably not even retarded. Billy F eventually went through Meds. Spud Arnetson never got higher than a C-minus in his life. They were both fairly normal kids. But Tom was eternally grateful to the redhaired security guy, subconsciously, that is, for the rest of his life.

Life goes on. Tom is still friends with Billy Flaherty several years later around college, but is never friends again with Spud Arnetson. Spud becomes a goof and a car thief, other boys are big on sports, as is Tom, basketball at least, and Tom and Billy both tend to be A students. Tom fits into Michael Of All Angels with a sudden classroom flair. He performs when the priest's back is turned. At home, he eats his mother's pasta with great gusto. He has erections, hard-ons, boners, because of his sister Francesca, often known simply as Fran to friends later on in high school. He gets surprisingly good marks in English (Italian he speaks at home, French he finds boring, Latin seems to amuse him, as if filling him with some enormous private joke: in fact, he and Billy F will often greet each other in the corridors of Bloor Collegiate years later or in the washrooms or the gym with various select and quite complicated Latin phrases, sometimes added to or stretched with phrases in Toronto pig-latin, sometimes just by themselves, *sui generis*, pure as the driven rain, etc.).

Billy Flaherty isn't the only close friend Tom makes as high school advances. There are other boys. Francesco, Frank, Abalone, also Italian, becomes a close associate. They are both interested in science. Abalone has a remarkably beautiful older sister, Dolores, who is lush and sardonic and precocious compared to Fran who is simply a very attractive "good girl." Martin Kemmel becomes a close friend. He lives over by Dovercourt Road. They play baseball together at Christie Pits in the summer. Tom hasn't

49

focused on basketball yet. He hasn't come into the last 4 inches of his height. The four of them plus several other boys, several girls: Knish, because she kisses like a potato, but who is attractive and lets him feel her breasts, bare, from swell to nipple, feeling swell, nipped indeed, in the Alhambra theatre; Bonny Rattigan, who is a tomboy but terrific, and goes everywhere by bicycle. The boys love seeing her approach, of course this isn't a winter memory, it's what will become a summer memory, but they also love watching her disappear, blond head down, bluejeaned buttocks a work of art oscillating above the blurred CCM spinning spokes. Who became a surgeon out of St. Michael's Hospital at the age of 26. Who masturbated Tom to orgasm in the tree house behind his friend Kemmel's. Who took him in her mouth. Who collected stamps, and prized the large triangular Ukrainian stamps because her first boyfriend in high school was of Ukrainian descent, dark, and name of William.

When Tom gets in trouble with Mr. Robertson over the burning textbooks question, it is Kemmel who comes to his aid and provides a foolproof alibi for him. When he fights Jake Dentner out in the schoolyard back in Grade 11 one afternoon out at the wide back of the school, hot sunsoaked gravel looking south over Dufferin Race Track, it is Billy F and Frank who move in and push Dentner's bulky older friends Bob Stewart and Al Kochins out of the way, saying, "Com'on, they can handle it. Mind your ass." And Kochins and Stewart had done exactly that. Minded their big asses.

Tom likes to have fun, likes to make his moves, is not conceited, not entirely inconsiderate, but he is fun-loving to excess and is always conscious of perfection. Perfection is a rising exhilaration like the red mercury in a barometer, which is another tower image perhaps. As an image perfection is always part of a juxtaposition that involves status, a form of height, after all. In other words, he is lazy in a sense, but is also competitive. Given to daydreaming, but not always sure of what to do when he is completely on his own. So it came to be said at Bloor Collegiate after Tom left, that for Tom Garrone perfection was something that came out of free flow, free fall, perhaps out of an almost oblivious intelligence, hitting and missing and then hitting again, hopefully to score a bullseye, gold ring, or whatever, but always striking out in the blue air as if to achieve something.

Another experience that happens to prevent Tom from simply evolving as a perfectly normal, slightly tall for his age high school student, is Cesar Pavese. Cesar Pavese is the great Italian writer of the late '30s and 1940s, a handsome, slightly weathered, slightly sardonic man with dark hair pushed back from his forehead and steel-rimmed glasses. He is a poet and a novelist. He isn't a Marxist, but he has basic political attitudes not that far from Marxism. He is a good writer and a compelling figure. Pavese comes to Tom in the form of a vision, or, to be fashionable, a sort of brief hallucination one afternoon while Tom is reading in the Gladstone Public Library.

Tom is walking over to the geography section to pull down a book on Africa, and he suddenly has an intense graphic sense of Pavese, whom his uncle has mentioned once or twice, whom his mother had seen at a cafe when she was in Rome for some reason, and whom Tom has read a couple of stories by; Pavese is in the library, standing between Tom and the shelves, hands in pockets, slightly rumpled, casual, an attractive man with a touch of bitterness emanating from the corners of his shapely mouth. Tom stands there in the library, transfixed, for at least 5 minutes. 5 minutes is a long time. It is to become one of the important recurring measures of time in Tom's life. 5 minutes is the length, before cutting down and arranging, of the first draft of the songs Tom will start writing at approximately age 27. It is also the maximum amount of time that he can devote to thinking about something that has nothing to do with himself.

What the Pavese incident means is that Tom suddenly decides he wants to be, eventually, when all the high school and basketball and immediate circumstances are over, a writer. Not like Pavese exactly, but a writer. Something, like Pavese.

This is a serious question because he knows even before he begins to read everything Pavese has written, including some work in Italian which he struggles through, it isn't available in English, that Pavese has committed suicide, not like his father who dies in an "industrial accident," and has therefore broken the Church's most serious taboo.

The Church, although Tom wasn't intensely religious, he was more religious, if anything, about the exact layout of the slam-dunk, could not denounce anything more severely. This is serious, sure, but it does not dim Tom's intense admiration for everything that Pavese has written in his short but brilliant life, or, for that matter, Tom's interest in the women, photographs even, who had loved Pavese.

Fools that they were.

So what did the bizarre incident described here with Spud and Billy Flaherty have to do with various other parts of Tom's developing life?

Girls, for example, food, surely it didn't change his appetite, or cars which he later collected, potency, planes, trains, ambition, his idea of history and incident, perhaps, or his enormous surge of feeling for that moment in Mahler's 1st when the horns begin to brood with sexual joy, like swans?

Girls were not Tom's problem in life. "Women," his uncle Giacomo once said to him "are like the flowers of the field." Tom thought this was pretentious. Giacomo smoked his cigar on the front porch at 246 Grace Street, although older Italian men don't usually smoke cigars. Giacomo was in business. Tom thought his uncle's view of women sounded like an older man who wants to look at a lot of girls on the street and admire their legs or their backs or their dresses. The girls Tom knew, and he thought largely in terms of the girls he actually knew, as well as the women he read about in books or magazines, were not very much like the flowers of the field. What field? What he knew was school. They were wild, shy, irascible, horny, hornier even than Tom at times, committed, uncommitted, vengeful, vivacious, exuberant, self-determined, but always attractive. They were challenging, some of them even talked about feminism. Sure, he thought sometimes, more jobs for women. How about for women like my aunt?

But they were not achievers in the sense that Tom, with his big DC 10 (forget the DC 10, if it's a Delta, it's a problem), with his big 727 Al Italia ego, was an achiever.

When he jumped for the basket and got the slam-dunk to break a tie in the middle of a game between Bloor and Riverdale, arch rivals, arch maniacs, for example, or when he got 99 in Geography which was a subject that fascinated him as literature, in its literary form, but bored him to tears as a classroom subject – then he was at the centre of a sort of blue sky where the sun seemed to be perpetually shining. The Spud Arnetsons of the world, or whoever it was at the back of his head, could not touch him. He lashed out with one large Nike-shod foot and Arnetson plummeted.

Tom loved Wendy Taylor, Bonny Armstrong, Helen Hrtanak, Joanna Murphy, Grace Solipstano, and Maria Gevalado. Loved them at various times wildly, into a confusion of sheets which slowly became an intense, almost white world of night and day combined.

Tom's view of himself as an athletic but fundamentally literary type will change, although naturally he can't foresee this as yet, probably after he meets the Desperados for the first time in a little bar down on the lower East Side in New York the Bad; but his interest in achievement and his inability to deal with it will continue. His desire to write great stories, about Life, his life in Toronto, the Italian community, Frank Alberfetti's vegetable store, Paolo Strematti cheating on his wife. That will change, that'll change.

But his confusion about women will probably remain the same. There will always be two of them. One fairly traditional, the other more post-modern than Gucci. Tom will romanticize both because they are women, because they were not at the Tower on the day of his mishap, but they were, in a sense, at home at 246 Grace Street when he arrived that day. So. He will romanticize both of them, and will often lie awake at night, his long body stretched out like an awkward swimmer, kicking the cool sheets into a world of white confusion.

But at home, at school where his friendships rapidly expand to include scores of boys his own age and older, sports-interested types and in a few cases, another poet or whatever such as he is himself, with girls, at the local YMCA on Dovercourt at College, Tom is a model guy. As he also is if they go out to the country southwest of the city to his cousin's farm, milking the occasional cow, fairly occasional, Tom is an easygoing guy, restless, smart, but with all this tension, or so it would appear, bottled up inside him somewhere, like a small green bottle, filled with helium perhaps, floating somewhere in the open space at the back of his head, like a small green bottle tossed from a ship in space by a careless astronaut.

He is a bit antsy about some things, occasionally strained by ambition, but the sort of kid who looks as if he may become successful and then fool everybody by suddenly deciding to give it all up. He is like that in school sometimes. He tackles a particular project with incredible deep silent concentration and then, when it is finished and successful he suddenly shows no more interest in the subject, although it is possible that he may think about it as a reference. Basketball is different. Basketball is a continual challenge. There is no limit to how good you can be at basketball.

Albertini Garrone, Tom's ample traditional mother, occasionally suggests that she can see Tom becoming extremely successful in business, she wants him to be a lawyer; for example she is convinced by the time Tom is in Grade 13 at Bloor Collegiate and thriving like a healthy plant that he should have a great career as a leading lawyer, a senator, even, maybe a member of government. She also sees him, for some obscure reason, as going into the steel business, perhaps in Hamilton. Mrs. Garrone has strange pictures of him in some of the different southern Ontario regions, and doing extremely well, making millions perhaps. Canada needs steel. There are opportunities. Most of the Anglo Canadians don't know fettuccine or carpaccio about how to make good steel. Simple. Because they don't have any traditions. This was, of course, because her brother, Hamilcar, had been in the steel business back in Italy, in Turin, as a matter of fact.

But Tom, romping through high school and considering college, finally chooses Harvard, which is impressed with his range of extra-curricular activities, writing, ab-ex painting, well, he did a painting once, not a lot, music, he plays mouth organ but lies and says piano and violin, the violin having of course been his father's (his father's passion, almost vocation, and eventual destruction – not of the man, per se, but of his stomach, his sense of frustration, the great Latin word *frustrere*, the sense of sadness turning black and bopping Giuseppe often on the side of the head like an angry mother as he left for work on cold Toronto winter white snow-swept mornings in the great frozen northern metropolis with his black lunchpail and his great thick chunky Italian rye and mortadella – which means death of woman – and tomato and cheese sandwiches); what else? Tom includes farming, nature walks, and soil analysis, also claims to be interested in becoming an ecological or more precisely pollenological expert on the history of the Scarborough Bluffs, that range of crumbling and rugged cliffs, bluffs, which slopes down from Scarborough at the east end of Toronto into the blue nothingness of Lake Ontario, where Tom sometimes sails with a friend, the son of a family whose father owns a construction equipment company but is rumoured to be *cosa nostra*. "Who isn't?" says Tom's friend bitterly, one afternoon as they eat their hamburgers out in the middle of blue Lake Ontario. "Who isn't?"

Giuseppe gives Tom 2 main gifts in life, besides love, of course, and besides his death, which hasn't happened yet, and which, when it does happen, will become a dark spot on Tom's computer screen in 4th year Harvard.

The first of these 2 gifts is Giuseppe Amadeus's dislike of music, his feeling that music betrayed him, the way some men are about women, perhaps; music had let him down like a faithless woman, a *strega*, in a red dress skittering off along the cobbles leading north from the sunlit piazza cafes of the San Borasino in Rome; as a city, his father's great love, the city itself, its greatness, its prestige, its history, its why not say it out loud here this afternoon in the bright sunlight, it's absolute like a Papal decree immortality. And so the father, Giuseppe Amadeus Garrone, had given up music, although he was not that bad a violinist, he just couldn't find very much in the way of gainful employment, being something of a village boy who had come to Rome from Tuscany in pursuit of love, amor, greatness, and perhaps even money, and had finally taken up the trade of a simple brick layer instead.

The second of these two primary gifts that his father passes on to Thomas Eduardo Garrone, otherwise known as The Stick, because he was so thin, tall, and slim some said; but his mother Mama Garrone said, Like a stick, he's so tall and thin. The second of these two primary gifts was his father's passionate belief, especially after they had come to America, well, no, not exactly America, but as his father was fond of saying, "Christopher Columbus, who was ours and who will always be ours, and Italian, so, therefore he's ours, he's not George Washington's, George Washington made the Revolution, but Christopher discovered America, he's not

55

Thomas Jefferson's, after whom Tom is named, he's ours, an Italian, like us, a wop, a dago, a good dago, a great el woppo with a big nose," Tom's father had an enormous nose, a real schnauzzo; but, as his father was also fond of saying, "Columbus didn't really discover what we now call America anyway," and therefore, as he would point out, holding up the big blue and white with fine yellow and red lines map of North America, "what difference does it make if we're here, in Toronto, where the majority of the good restaurants and tailor shops and small building companies are Italian anyway, or, for example," he would beat the table with the big baguette of crusty Calabrese bread they cut slices from on the breadboard in the middle of the table, "if we're down here in New York, where your cousin Sal and his wife live and those *battaschardi* they've got for children; or, for example," he would move his big square-bottomed wine glass around the table like a Columbian compass, "if we live over here where the boy's (the boy was Tom of course) uncle Giambattista lives in New Jersey with that huge fat ugly woman from Lombardy who tricked him into marrying her just because she was 6 months in the family way and her father owns a hardware business and wanted very much, especially when his daughter couldn't do the family dishes any more because she was as I've said 6 months, not 6 weeks, but 6 months, *apregnento*. Ah. What difference, eh, this is all America."

And his father, all 6'2" of him with flat sloping chest, the big long arms and that wide sloping but outwards belly sitting there in the kitchen with its bright yellow lights on Grace Street and Tom had been God, Jesus, how old at that time, he must have been 4 or 5 at the most and his father would sigh with pleasure with relief with relaxation at the good spaghetti and vitello that his mother had prepared and fold up the map and put it away and consider the object lesson taught and the matter in general more or less closed and committed to passionate belief.

So Tom had this considerable sense of family, Italian past, close-knit neighbourhood, leafy maple & ash trees background, much more so than he had a very clear concept of anything Canadian.

Of course a lot of different things affected Tom's development and therefore could be called the "groundwork" of the kaleidoscope of events that happened to him as late as 1978. School, reading Jean-Paul Sartre without wearing tinted glasses, a little trouble at customs one year to do with some hash brownies. Nothing serious.

But probably the biggest thing underlying Tom's sense of ascent and fear of descent, his vestige of volatility from being at the top of the CN Tower, was his affection for his family and their life, and the enormous influence of his grandfather, Albertini's father, who can't be discussed here for various reasons, who spoke to Giuseppe Amadeus the *III*, and implored him to give his first son a new name, which is why Giuseppe had called Tom "Tomaszo," just to make a difference in the Garrone family lineage.

Light-hearted and sombre by turns, high school leads to college, and Tom's first change of city (since Orillia) is going to be Boston. Boston means Cambridge, Mass., where he has been accepted by Harvard.

Previously, going down to the Canadian East Coast for summer holidays or out to B.C., he has always taken trains. Canadian trains. Those 1940s pale imitations of the first great trains of the Canadian north. No longer kept up. No longer a big investment of government or private industry. He has always taken trains. Written a couple of stories about trains as a matter of fact, unpublished, he remembers, in Grade 12 or maybe 11. Sometime back then. When his uncle suggested Tom come back to Italy with him for June and July one year, Tom was nonplussed. No trains. It seemed to be his one weakness, apart from trig and calculus.

College makes him fly, or something does and it's easy. As easy as drinking a different kind of orange juice. The bucolic pleasures of high school are over. Tom makes the move to the telephone one afternoon, before going to Harvard for registration, picks it up almost casually, reserves an economy flight one-way to Boston. And that's that. Tom's ready for travel. It was simple. After registration and settling in, Tom will get on the basketball team (although he isn't *really* more serious about basketball than he is about literature, he just likes to say he is), as 2nd string right forward: the basketball team flies to some of their engagements. There is nothing to it. He suddenly seems to take it all for granted.

The last link or thread to that dark pool of subconsciously compart-mentalized terror is neatly broken and tossed away, almost casually, like a used Kleenex.

Tom flies to Boston and flies home at holiday periods, unless he is invited somewhere else. He flies to New York for weekends sometimes, although he usually takes a train for the sake of economy. Mastering trig was, despite his high voltage IQ, fairly difficult for the calf. Abstractions aren't his piano forte. But flying, flying is even easier than making coffee. He doesn't have much money at college, not like some of the rich blond boys who buy their boxer shorts at Saks, or whose mothers buy their boxer shorts at Saks, whichever. But he will have money later, as it turns out. Some years later. After he begins writing songs.

Once, quite drunk after a late supper, too much bourbon after the beer and hamhocks they'd had together at an outdoor café on Murphy, west of Jackson, walking down a small side street in Kansas City, Mo., a cathedral of some size and some historic shading came up in front of Tom almost as suddenly as a passerby. "St. James," he said, out loud to himself, thinking of gothic King Street in Toronto, putting out one hand as if to ward it off, "St. James Cathedral Blues." Although that isn't the exact title of the song, at all. But it wasn't the same cathedral anyway and he was a little drunk that night. He didn't remember the incident clearly, went back to the hotel and slept till 10 a.m. or so, until several days later at which time it struck him as simply amusing, like an odd postcard, or an anecdote someone had told him about a friend.

September, 1977, Diggers are no longer turning up in San Francisco get-ting haircuts but keeping their wide-brimmed hats. Tom saw them too. Tom saw them on television, and he saw them in LIFE magazine and in Union Square. "Ah, what would America be without LIFE magazine?" he says to a pustuled blond young customs guy a week later at Boston Airport. "I just watch football," says the pustuled kid, "how long are you staying in Boston?" "I'm at college," says Tom, "I'm staying forever, for years, anyway."

He goes first to New York, and then to Boston to attend Harvard, which he has chosen, partly for its proximity to New York, for its crusty longevi-ty and because of its English Department. He goes expecting beer, skittles, profundity, post-structuralism, uplifted plaid skirts, lampoons, study hours, but also, he hopes, the right beginnings for himself as a writer. Perhaps he may become the Italian Chekhov, he isn't sure. He is up for it, and anything seems possible.

Tom loves flying. Birds fly. Rickenbacker had flown, and waved to America from the cockpit of a bi-plane as he flew past. Lindbergh had flown and waved to the cold North Atlantic as he flew past, waved to icebergs perhaps. Amelia Earhart had flown and crashed in Nova Scotia once, as a matter of fact. Tom has been to Nova Scotia. Tides and lobsters. He caught fish there. Tom flies. Tom loves flying. He likes the 40,000' altitudes. It makes him think of Dante, whom Tom loves, although Tom is Canadian, well, from Toronto; he is more at home with Truman Capote and Mark Twain than with William Davis. In the same bed or railway coach, or whatever. He packs 1 suitcase and the 1958 battered Olivetti Underwood office model typewriter, gets on an Air Canada 727 and flies first to New York and then to Boston, home of flags, museums, bluefish, and where you get scrod.

Life is effortless. He even drinks on the plane. Sitting with his long legs crossed awkwardly in the tight space, as comfortable as a big Italian seagull. He feels slightly intimidated, glancing over his magazines, *Time*, *Esquire*, *Newsweek*, that he may have difficulty with some of the pass courses in Harvard English, philosophy, for example. He doesn't realize, looking down at the enormous expanse of bright sunlit shimmering grey-blue Atlantic, that the courses will be a snap, a rooster, a piece of cake. He doesn't realize, there is some inherent modesty in Tom despite his breeziness, what options *will* turn out to be difficult. He will probably *not* become the Italian Chekhov. Chekhov was Russian, after all. Things have their place in the world. Tom's place in the world is to be a serious and innocent clown, a kind of big and awkward, except on the basketball court, *polpaccio*. The 727 is something neither Shakespeare nor Ariel could have conceived. Life is effortless. Tom has not yet gone seedy on the lower East Side; and, of course, not even had an intimation of Chuck Berry or a hint of Woody Guthrie. He still hasn't met up with the Desperados, or with demondrummer Bats, or with Whitney.

        Sean Young's eyes shine out at you like huge orbs
of light.
      She is in a pensive mood this afternoon. You feel
you've known her for years,
             since college,
maybe since high school. She was in a gleeful mood for several days
after the story about gluing James Woods' penis to his thigh
with Crazy Glue,
        but that's all stale gossip now,
it probably didn't happen anyway. What was Woods sleeping
on a bench out in the lot in the nude for anyway? Who knows?
We make up stories so that we can have a map involving people.
There are so many stars in the sky it would take you a lifetime
to memorize their different names. Some are 1000 light years
away, some are 5000 light years away,
                they are really just small
bits of rock
      like bits of the Rocky Mountains,
              bits of the Sierra
Madre
    floating grey [black from a distance
              & burning with reflected
light] & mysterious in the luminous blue light of outer
space. My friend Virgo's first name is Sean, no
resemblance
      although he does have large blue eyes. Hers are a sort
of golden hazel,
      making for various allusions perhaps, reflections
in a golden eye, the golden bowl, put a little sugar [what is that
a reference to? cocaine, come in me, which? are you sure?]
                    Elizabeth Taylor

has violet eyes & walks nude up the living room staircase in
the Carson McCullers film, Brando playing an army captain
confused & beautiful as usual & having trouble with the horses,
the horses restless as hell.

One of Lester Young's most beautiful solos
is
"I Can't Give You Anything but Love." I can't. Give
you anything.
But love has a way of lifting up
on the soft currents of a summer wind & behaving inappropriately
like a red kite. The cigarette smoke is hazy
& the tall black man lifts the saxophone as if he wants
to fly right through the timbered ceiling
of this small Pennsylvania road house.
My mother is sitting
at a table about ½ way down the room. It's hot. My father
has gone to the washroom the MENS to wash his face
& probably give his moustache a quick brush with his hand.
It is 1936
& they are on vacation. Roosevelt has been
in the White House for a long time now. The cars are blunt
& they are mostly dark colours.
Roosevelt's friend Mackenzie King has been in Ottawa
for years. The unemployed workers move across Ontario
in stained work pants & dark suit jackets
with a scarf, but not in summer when they sleep out in parks
& on the lawns of city halls.
Early morning sunlight
on the Pennsylvania Turnpike all those blunt dark cars
moving in a serious line look ½ surreal. Raymond Chandler
is beginning another novel. There are huge food lines
in Pittsburgh. My mother & father have money but are not
always kind to each other. He winks with one dark eye
jauntily. My mother smiles
unconsciously tapping her thick wedding band on the formica
table top. I can't give you anything but love.

MY EMMA GOLDMAN T-SHIRT

Do you remember that light beige Emma
Goldman t-shirt you gave me one summer?
My friend Susan
Berlin was married to Jeremy Larner for a while
who wrote "Drive, He Said," taking his title
from a poem by Robert Creeley about the darkness that wafts across
the highways of life
great billows of it, well, okay, her 12-year-old
son Jesse was sitting in the living room propped up against the wall
one afternoon reading volume 1 of *The Memoirs Of Emma
Goldman*, notes from the 1920s, & I said, Okay, that's cool.

Anyway the t-shirt, it gets a lot of attention, it says,   IF I CAN'T DANCE
I DON'T WANT TO BE
PART OF YOUR REVOLUTION. Her picture in large
black solids is in the middle of the slogan. People have to bend over
on the street to pick out exactly who she is – steel-rim glasses
& beautiful, & of course she's all in black on the t-shirt, she looks
as if she should be carrying an umbrella walking along some beach
in Germany in the 1890s. It's a good shirt, & I thought I'd write
you a note & say thanks for it.
I'm very widely read
but I'm more of a Tom Stoppard Edward Said social anarchist now
& I don't usually carry a black umbrella. But you know what they
say – "Anarchists come in different forms." And when you look
into my face you can see it all very clearly.
It's a loose
comfortable shirt & I wear it casually like a young rock&roll kid
wearing a t-shirt that says   N I R V A N A.

The white
skins
are the white skinheads, shaven clean as a baseball,
you've seen them around, also
called pinheads. The
red skins
are the socialists, they're the ones who came first,
same height & weight etc. but they have red shoe laces
in their boots – black military highcuts,
that's what they all wear,
very much like std US military
combat issue. It's confusing as hell, isn't it? And then
over here we've got ska heads
& the occasional artist
or Park Avenue photographer
who decides to shave his head. I guess they're all working
class youth who like tavern culture & this is a fad. Some
of them are unemployed, probably none of the white skinheads
like Tangerine Dream
or Uta Lempur very much, or Brecht,
for example, no, Brecht wouldn't be very popular. The red
skinheads probably don't read Brecht either, various brands
of Löwenbrau are popular or unpopular but the red skinheads
defend the rights of Turkish *guestarbeiters*,
& the white
skinheads seem to like fire bombs.

> I can see him travelling by bus
with the orchestra
> from Toronto to the Muskokas
to entertain vacationers & summer residents. My friend
Colin Simpson's parents heard him at a lake resort
somewhere east of Parry Sound in the early 40s. The war
was on, Colin's father,
> a major stockholder
in Massey-Harris [tractors, combines, threshers],
was drunk, the mood of the evening was lively
according to Colin's memory. Hamilton,
> Windsor [across from Detroit],
but mostly the Muskokas &, of course, Toronto – Palais Royale,
the Imperial Room at the Royal York Hotel,
places like that. Granted, he went Hollywood,
& granted, he only does concerts now, & he can't sing any more
anyway. But "Full Moon, Empty Arms" [he was quite young then],
now that's an Ontario song.
> "My Foolish Heart" – that's mature
Frank Sinatra, better than the young crooner,
but he's still got his chops, sharp articulation, dramatic interpretation
some of those neat tricks like singing ½ a beat off.
He was good before he turned 41,
> or 42,
> he had moves,
& then he moved further south & he stopped doing the bars.
It was nothing but concert tours, & The Sands Hotel in Las Vegas.
Let me tell you something – I liked him in *Man With the Golden
Arm*. He was good,
> playing the thin, intense, pale musician
[definitely an *east* Ontario guy] coming off heroin,

& the scene where Kim Novak wearing a sweater I can only describe
as risqué by its very intention
                              lying on top of him
with a blanket to keep him warm, he's going cold turkey,
he hasn't had a shot for days & he's got the chills,
boy, that was a great scene. Even now,
                                        standing in Ontario,
looking as far south as Texas [where they have been having
a lot of trouble – Killeen, Tex., where the guy drove his truck
through the window of the restaurant & shot 23 people; Waco, Tex.,
where the ATF laid seige to the compound of the Branch Davidians
& approx. 63 people were killed, that's trouble],
                                        even now,
I like "I've Got the World on a String," the bravura
of the upbeat is like wild ducks flying across Point Pelee, Ont.

He said, "I've been trying to keep the baby
Jesus
out of my mind for years."
I'm in the back seat,
don't look at me, I'm not the baby Jesus.
I'm about 20, we're all about 20,
I'm drinking coffee out of a red plastic thermos cup.
I think,
Funny, I've never thought of Jack
as a Christian kind of guy, certainly not a holy roller.
We're working at Kelvinator for a few weeks.
I'm reading the *Toronto Star* in the back seat
& Morris says, with that woodchuck chuck in his voice,
"Well he won't help you win any money at the races."
And that's true, I think to myself.
The baby Jesus won't bring Sailor's Rest into the wire ahead of the field.
I'm not really thinking at all very much, I'm tired.
Overtime last night but they gave it to someone else tonight.
Jack & Morris haven't had any all this week.
Had a couple of drinks after lunch,
we were working on big white door assemblies. They began to look
like images from the Apollo flights. I could see Armstrong walking
on the moon and carrying a door assembly on his shoulder.
I smack Morris on the back of the head with my newspaper.
"Jesus is all about love," I tell him.
Dead skunk by the shoulder as we exit from the 401
and drop down a couple of streets to get onto Morningside
Drive. It was hot, what was a skunk doing on the 401 anyway? There
were small insects, hot delicate dark
gnats squashed across the dusty blue windshield.

"Avanti, avanti," she says, pushing the little
boy in the blue cap,
                    he looks about 9½ or 10,
up the scuffed dusty marble steps of Union Station
onto the cement platform
                         where the Toronto Express
to Buffalo is about to leave. There are
giant orange&blue weather balloons moving at a slow
northeasterly pace over Pickering,
                                  a small community
airport some 34 miles away. Avanti. She has a suitcase in one
hand & a big 1940s purse & a laundry bag bulging with
I don't know what in her left hand. There are different trains in America.
The designs change from time to time. This is one of the great CP trains.
Some are classics & some aren't. "Avanti,
                                        avanti," she says,
& cuffs him on the ear. He
is straining up on his toes with the huge suitcase
as the train comes in. When she cuffs him he laughs
& leans back in her direction as if she were a large tree
in dark blue sweaters and a rumpled black skirt suit
with black stockings.

October explodes in this (wooded) hilly & potato rich enclave at the northern end of the Niagara escarpment. Alliston, on the Nottawasaga, & other towns west to Orangeville are warm & soft & gusty this Friday, 7:35 a.m. Orange and blue umbrellas on front porches, rain slickers out on the farms. Everywhere you look the trees have gone as berserk as a loon's hypothalamus with riots of orange yellow red pale vermilion savagely oversweet turned on itself crimson dark. There is a fine October rain coming down, so fine that you can hardly see it, almost a mist, it barely wets your face. 16°. A few 40 mph ducks skim the tops of distant lush wet trees. Geese crossing in loose Vs down by the bridge. This is western Ontario but continentally almost as far south as Massachusetts, Point Pelee, or Frank Lloyd Wright's Chicago. The air is full of oxygen. The dense rich colours swim in this air like Matisse nudes, blue knees & elbows, magenta buttocks. Warm thick air gives a tremendous lift to your motion. I seem to fly above the pale dark grey early morning towns of soft hills & steeples almost like Chagall's crazy mystical Rabbi fiddling over the scant roofs of pre ww 1 Minsk. (1000s of miles north of where Babel wrote about Itzak the gangster. Where Gurdjieff sold the barrel of bad herring and put the money into fresh animal skins.) Water trickles gently along the curbs into the cosy black gratings of innumerable sewers. It's warm & wet & gorgeous. My Rockports squelch on the gravel. I lift my face up to the sky. I open my black umbrella. I wave to you happily my friends across the shimmering slopes of the western escarpment.

I said
[it was about 7:30
& there was a pool of darkness at 34th & Avenue B]
[there was a yellow taxi, I had said the corn chowder needed more
chicken stock]
to my friend Adam Gopnik
who is, for sure, no average GOP kind of guy, "You stay in New
York & write for the *New Yorker*. And I will go back to Toronto,
that big sprawling city on the north shore of Lake Ontario,
& I will have a huge empty white room & corn chowder with chorizo
sausages
& I will move Tom (Bass) from chapter 7 to chapter 9,
& I will write a Matisse blue spotlight song
& you will be in the song, wearing an old sweat with 'Williams'
across the grey front,
writing about Matisse." "How can you compare Murray Schafer
to Philip Glass?" "You can't, they're too different. I like
Schafer's 'Northern String Quartets,' but there's not very much loon
in them." New York is a dying city. But I really like the way
people shoot each other in Sam Peckinpah films. You might as well
write a short history of sound poetry in which you say they all seem
to have been influenced by television dubs. But not me. I would
rather go home & listen to African boat songs   & think
about that slow hot butter soft sun   & paddling down a river
of infinity.

Postmoderns like things to be laid out calmly
& precisely like design components on a large drawing board.
Like Robert Smithson's Earthworks, for example. Earth & works –
postmodernism is gutsier than people think. Mississippi
earth is swampy as you get south of Oxford down to the gulf.
I don't like F's *Absalom, Absalom!* very much. I don't like the way
it begins with the runaway slave. F himself is very present,
but in a confused sort of way – splashes of author colour come
through but seem disparate. It's like a camera falling
through the narrative & it doesn't work. The characters don't tell their
     own stories
explicitly or implicitly.
Ask any of your friends about their favourite Faulkner
characters and they'll probably say, Popeye,
Temple Drake, Jason, Caddy, the barn-burning father. Claes Oldenburg's
giant hamburgers take us back to the 50s. Faulkner was young
in the 20s. And was then smacked in the face
with the 30s & the Depression. I'm probably being unfair
to this book. I'm reading in a sunny room and listening
to Wynton Marsalis's solos on a CD with Kathleen Battle
who is singing up a rich dark storm & Wynton, it's Handel, is
right there as if he had written the music himself. Sure
there is probably a point of view from which you could enjoy
Absalom, Absalom! I don't know, I sort of like the title.
But not as much as *Light in August* or the story of Jason & Caddy.
Marsalis goes up into C & I toss the book over on the couch
& watch the small English sparrows & the grey squirrel
outside my front windows on this cool blue May afternoon. The
title's interesting, isn't it? *Absalom, Absalom!* It sounds
too biblical for the 1930s of Huey Long.

I have a green & yellow plastic Tonka dump
truck
on the left side of my double sink in the kitchen.

Imagine that? An adult white male writer who studies
Wittgenstein
& he's got
a child's toy
that he keeps in his kitchen sink.

Her name was Mayonnaise Dutton
& Tom loved her
& he lusted after her panties. Her panties
were cute
& she was pretty goddamn cute herself. But she didn't give a shit
about Tom.

When I look into the wide open cavity of my mouth
in the large hallway mirror it looks like a caricature
of Baudelaire's abyss. Don't misunderstand me. I don't mean
I have a whale in my mouth. No Jungian references to Melville.
I just mean it's so huge & pink & clean & wholesome. And innocent.
I'm an American outlaw & I have my whims. Lots of Hathaway shirts,
no Kenzo ties.
I don't have a lot of money. I'm actually quite
aggressive at times. I like to run water over the truck
in the morning while I do a few dishes, make coffee,
listen to the morning arts news
before I sit down to write for the day.

Hayden Washington Jones, 6'5", close-cropped hair, choco-late satiny skin, quiet, at times almost mordant. A tall guy, for sure, taller than Tom Garrone, and blocky, not tall and thin like Tom. In addition to which Hayden had an immeasurably greater knowledge of music than Tom possessed, and had never been even faintly tempted to write stories (although Hayden had stories, but he was a quiet amused kind of guy in regard to conversation) in the manner, although he had lived in Paris for a while and had driven a little Peugeot minor, of some French guy like Albert Camus.

Hayden had been an A student at Jefferson High School in Brooklyn, a scholarship student, music obsessive, tight end distinguished for broken field play at Yale in the late 60s, a music compulsive, Juilliard in New York, and then Paris in 1974.

His mother was a school teacher and a regular churchwoman. His older sister Dahlia was the neighbourhood beauty in their part of Brooklyn, and a bit of a sass and also a bit of a snoot, she could look down her nose at a school teacher or a bank manager with equal ease. But she sang in the church choir and when she sang she was a somewhat different kind of sister.

Anyway, first song, as in first love, first sex, first time bareback, first time driving home from Jones Beach, not that his family owned it, nobody owns Jones Beach, although it isn't really public property either. Hayden Jones wrote his first song when he was about 11 years old. It wasn't a bad song. It was a song about playing tag with his brother. It was a 4-bar blues. And who knows, maybe it was about his sister. It wasn't about his mother, and it wasn't about Jesus. His mother said it was a good song. His father didn't say anything. His father was at the race track in Detroit, Dee/troite, hanging out with Fox & Masters & Wilberson & Lapointe. It was a pretty good song for a boy who was already 5'10", handsome enough to be noticed on the street, LaFayette & Lancaster, and hadn't started showing any interest in girls as yet. It was a pretty good song with his own melody and he did the harmonic himself both vocally and on the family living room piano. But he didn't write another song or even think about writing songs again until he was about 27. He was a little older than the rest of the Desperados, the black / white blues band he helped to form after coming back from Paris, where he knew Tom Garrone from, where he knew Stash and the others. He was about 4 years older, and as far as music was concerned he was a lot smarter, but he didn't go around saying so. Hayden was a composer, blues-based and a Bartok obsessive, and unlike most composers he was hooked up with a hard line, flat out band that was about to take America by storm, if they would listen to him, that is. He wasn't, when Tom Garrone met him, walking around in a loft whistling scores to himself, although he sometimes did that as well.

Juilliard followed Yale. Hayden had been playing with groups and arranging, becoming an arranger as well as a brilliant keyboards player, but arranging was definitely his first and greatest love supreme, and had been since he was around 15.

It was amazing that he never worried about his hands when he played football. First at Jefferson, then at Yale. At Yale more seriously, because *it* was more serious; for example, these guys at Yale were tough, really tough. They were nothing like Yale boys doing their M.A.s in philosophy and having a sandwich and a beer at Cookie's, a familiar sandwich place for lunch, booths and all, in New Haven. Uh, uh. They were tough.

But Hayden never worried about his hands when he played football, and he never worried about his mind. He didn't joke around with the older guys in the locker room that much, not especially, not so you would notice, Hayden was very contained, again, not very much like Tom who is tall and thin and likeable, but at times a bit of a schlemiel, a sincere guy but a guy who babbles a bit too much.

Hayden lived in a garrett, well, a third-floor maid's room, when he studied in Paris. Not quite like Erik Satie, to whom Hayden's heart belonged absolutely, although he was not to follow in Satie's direction. He lived on croque monsieurs and cheap hamburger meat from a little Algerian butcher down the rue. So when he first met Tom in the spring of 1976, Bats brought this tall pale Italian guy with a huge smile into Dempster's where they were eating after a rehearsal, down on the Lower East Side, he was immediately sympathetic because he thought of himself living in the cold third-floor maid's room in Paris.

Following this pace, which was really more a scheduled pace than he really wanted, his feelings about music were pretty wide and handsome, and free and full of initiative. He came back to New York a little restless and wound up doing more work than he really wanted, for NBC and ABC, which is when he first met up with the Desperados.

Hayden loved the funk of jazz, and the history of European music. He had been named after a great German composer, whom his father had picked up a book about almost by accident, when he was in one of his reading phases, trumpet, reading, lamplight, bourbon and burnout, off to horses and Fox & Wilberson. But Hayden's father, at that point in time, 31 years ago, knew fields of sweet peas about arranging, knew fields of sweet yams and tobacco about the history of music, European included, historical or otherwise, compared to what his brilliant son Hayden came to know, even some bits and pieces from contemporary South American, although those bossa nova and bossa samba trips were not really Hayden's specialty.

So Hayden Washington Jones, 29 at the time, about 4 years older than the other members of the Desperados and much more experienced, in matters of music at least, in matters of composition and genre, half note and full note, harmonic shading and harmonic disruption, continued his daytime work for NBC and ABC, and gave up most of his evening freelance stuff, including an interesting film offer. He became the resident keyboards player and resident arranger for the Desperados. They numbered 7 at that time because Tom had not yet become a member of the group, nor had Tom yet introduced Whitney to the group. And Yvonne had not yet come into the group to do her fabulous one-of-a-kind, Detroit back-up turned-around R&B background vocals.

"I could have a nice tight," he reflected, "little quartet of my own." He said this to Tom out of the blue, and it was a very blue day outside, golden, they were going through Kansas, on the tour bus one afternoon. "Cool," said Tom, and Hayden smiled sideways at him, scrunched a little in the expanded seat. "But then we'd be playing small clubs and I wouldn't be changing the conventions of large music." So that was Hayden's dream.

"My man," Tom said, and Hayden leaned over in the cramped quarters of the seat and slapped him gently on his dimpled chin.

Satie was often one of his main concerns, but most of his jazz friends in New York thought he took Satie too seriously. So after a few sessions together, Hayden helped to form the Desperados, about a year before Tom came along, and apart from the occasional disagreement with Stash, for example, the results were really powerful. He played a major role on keyboards, but more importantly, he wrote everything they played. There were some furrowed brows from time to time, Stash would shake his head, but he would get into it, Stash could play a wicked Stratocaster, Mason would shrug once in a while and say, "I can't play this." But, then he would. They were all very good musicians, and they came through for him.

"Go, white boy, go," he said under his breath, at the keyboards, in the middle of a concert one night as Stash was lunging out at the very girders of the place with some really impassioned improvisation. And Stash, even though he was lost to the world, black leather pants and a t-shirt that said SAVE THE SOUTH, not the usual blue denim garb favoured by the Desperados, and was in the middle of this deep solo, heard him, even though he said it under his breath. Impossible of course, men are supposed to believe in miracles, because they both wore earplugs. Most of the time, they did. Stash caught his eye a few chords later, and he smiled.

When Hayden was 15, which was a turning point, he was at a neighbourhood basement one day after school. There were some friends, older, and a couple of girls. One of the boys, Jaime, had a small envelope of white powder. Shit, there wasn't even very much in the envelope, just a little corner.

Four or five of them took a small snort each, and they wanted Hayden to try it. Hayden was younger, he was 15, but he had big status partly because he was such a good high school football player.

"No way, man," he said, "no way."

"Chicken, the football player's a chicken," one of the older boys said, and a couple of the others picked up the word, repeating it or changing it to sissy or baby.

"It won't bust your gut," said Jaime, "you don't want to do it because of your sport."

And Hayden had said, "No, it's not because I'm an athlete, it's because of my music." He associated getting high with not being able to play as well as he wanted to play.

Later that day, in the evening, he was at home sitting in the kitchen doing some math homework. His mother was out at a public school meeting. He had the big radio in the living room turned up loud, listening to it on and off as he worked.

He was about half-way through his work when he heard some German soprano, he didn't catch her name, sing Mozart's amazing aria where the young knight, a sacrificial figure, goes off to meet his death, but first says goodbye to three different people.

After the aria was over, he sat staring at the table. The radio was still on, it was loud, but he couldn't hear a thing. When he looked at the sheets of paper in front of him on the table, the sheets seemed to be blank. Then he lit a cigarette, he hardly ever smoked, but his mother had left a package sitting on the table. And when he looked back down at the table, the blank sheets seemed to be alive with muscular and lazy musical notes.

There was his friendship with Tom, for example, how they complemented each other in different ways, how these two guys, one 27, one 31, one white, Italian, the other black, from Brooklyn, both into music, Hayden much more so, but both into music, the two of them were wildly different in certain ways as individuals. But they complemented each other and were at many times, without being sentimental about this kind of thing in life between people, a bulwark for each other and a sounding board. Hayden with his street smart attitudes was very much alive and open to the world. But this openness was often closed behind a cool polite exterior as far as easy perception might be concerned. Hayden often spoke from a weight of academic courses, his exact reaching for the perfect note, speaking French, speaking, basic vocabulary, a little German, switching in his speaking of American English from Sam Adams to southern drawl, from Boston to a New York downtown accent to a voice that was a little gruffer, perhaps, but delicately, unpredictably shaded with a French phrase.

There was also the fact that Hayden never really got along with Stash, the player, a southern senator's son, for Christ's sake, he had first helped to form the Desperados, after meeting him at a party uptown somewhere; and Henner, the older guy, and ex-con, some people said, they had taken on as manager, sharp, very sharp. He didn't like Henner very much but didn't have anything specifically against him. And Whitney, of course, Whitney became a sort of garden of hanging flowers of Ur for Hayden, something to admire gruffly and almost indifferently from a distance, and close up, be outwardly very calm and avuncular. Like Tom's girlfriend, Whitney, Hayden was better-educated than the other guys, although Hayden, tight end, 6'5", solid, black, had obviously not gone to Vassar; he had however gone to Yale and Juilliard, so he was like a professor, a fellow player, a distant often humorous musical genius and a friend.

His friendship with Tom was more general and full of huge open spaces where they would talk, with only a few tokes of a single joint perhaps, and only a drink or two of bourbon, although the other Desperados drank like fish, maybe some coffee and they would talk long into the night after a concert that had gone well but left them with a variety of ideas to shuffle.

One of the things they talked about, naturally, Tom and Hayden sitting up late maybe in Hayden's room or maybe in Tom's, Whitney off drinking with someone, Mason off to sleep early, Swift, in Sacramento at least, out at the old town Reservoir with two redheads, he hadn't believed his good luck, he loved redheads and he loved two women at once, "Two redheads is two many women," said Hayden, but whatever, sitting up late, a few tokes each on one joint, maybe just two drinks each with tons of ice, that sort of thing, one of the things that Tom and Hayden talked about sometimes was how Tom wrote songs, which Tom did naturally, unconsciously, almost spontaneously, in an easy way that he could never possibly, despite however much frustration, duplicate when he wrote stories, fiction, what the class writers wrote, literature, you know, lit terr atchoore, this pain, that was important: and how Hayden wrote music, arranged music, knew where to put the horns, knew how to start off in one time signature and develop a certain kind of rhythm turning into melody and guitar-dominated back-beat, and then suddenly turn the whole thing over to keyboards and sonic percussion.

Tom's songs, brilliant scribbles really, were nothing without Hayden's arrangements, without Hayden's use of the French Horn on "Summer Cottage & Skunks," a new Tom song, then where would Tom be? Tom made his respect and admiration very evident; but what wasn't evident, not always at least, was Hayden's intense interest in how Tom wrote songs like "Summer Cottage & Skunks," or any other song for that matter. Because Hayden, who could have become a greater composer than the original Haydn, really longed at times to write songs as well, not that it was his main longing, his main longing was obviously music, music, pure music, pure music of a certain kind, what would later be called a "new American avant-garde."

But these were subjects Hayden had to lay aside more than he had planned after he began to tour with the Desperados. And it wasn't because of Whitney, by any means, or, as in Tom's case, because of the influence of his father. It was simply that he didn't have enough time. That big word that, after what happened in Texas, came to mean a lot to Hayden.

Music, time, and various things Hayden associated with his mother, who loved Hayden's work, not just because she was his mother, but who always preferred, just to be honest, certain Gospel songs, like "Will the Circle Be Unbroken?" and "We Shall Gather at the River," and "Swing Low," and "Joshua at the Battle of Jericho." And certain Broadway musical songs, even that somewhat broad comic song from *South Pacific*, "There Ain't Nothing Like a Dame," or "Porgy's Song," from *Porgy and Bess*. Songs she had grown up with, sung in church in some cases, that she preferred to the brilliant and explosive music that her most talented and oldest son wrote while he was with the Desperados.

And afterwards, after, for example, they put Hayden in prison for three years for somewhat brutally murdering, killing, it wasn't premeditated, old redcheeks ratshit Henner, their fallible and mendacious manager, then there was time, to think about the angularity of unexpected chords. And to reflect on the fact that Satie is a great composer, but "Will the Circle ..." is also a great song.

But that's another story, and of a somewhat different colour, or, as the French say, *couleur*. *Couleur, couleur,* the bitter fruit of my vengeance is mercy, saith the Lord, or maybe that's what the road and freight trains have to say.

We've been getting Dutch tomatoes at Loblaws
all summer long this year. They cost about 10¢ more
per tomato,
              but they're a lovely dark red, crimson,
they're almost blood red, no splash of green, *geogstadt*,
no rough marks or punctures,
                              they're hot house
but ripened on the vine, & I buy 4 or 5 of them
plus a snatch of dark green vine and put them on the kitchen
table.
       Tama Janowitz was cute,
she wasn't Dorothy Parker's big blonde
with a coarse realistic laugh and a high IQ; she's small
& petite & dark
                with an enormous blowsy mass of dark hair
& a squeaky voice & she wrote a bad splash-of-consciousness
novel about New York called
                       Slaves of New York,
the title was catchy, she probably got it from a 40s film,
but there was nothing realistic about the book after all.
Bart Simpson's view of Brad Pitt? I don't think Bart
Simpson has any view of Brad Pitt, Bart is just a cartoon
figure, not in Jules Feiffer's league, that you watch
while you eat some hot buttered popcorn. Nobody hears anything
about Tama Janowitz any more, but the Dutch tomatoes come all
the way from Holland & they're good & fresh & sweet
but they lack the character of the Ontario vine-ripened field tomato
with its stake marks & splashes of field sweet pale green.

Lake Simcoe afternoons. That was his story
about why we broke up. My story
is that he wanted sex every night & when he didn't get it
he would be up early in the morning
walking around in the kitchen with nothing on but a t-shirt,
blond pony tail slapping against his back,
dark patch of frown between his sweet blue eyes,
making good dark coffee
& standing there with his dick slapping against his thigh
being brusque. "How did you sleep?" How didja? As if it's
just a question of sex
& physical exercise like sports
or swimming;
    attentive, sure,
& self-indulgent & moody.

Of course that's what I loved about him, his boyishness, how
he would sit at the dinner table with one hand loose
between his legs, elbow of the other arm resting
on the table while he ate,
    talking excitedly,
the collar of his J. Peterson blue houndstooth checked shirt
that I don't think Thos. Jefferson actually wore
pushed back against the side of his neck.

I used to come home from a film
or a play
        by somebody like Genet or Ionesco
when I was in college – 4th year, English Lang & Lit –
& my roommate
                a big tall moody guy with red hair
from southern Manitoba, loves basketball, ice cream & girls,
would be sitting at his blond study desk with all the lights
on & at least a dozen books spread out on the floor –
every single book,
Ulysses by James Joyce, Women in Love by D.H. Lawrence,
would be opened at the appropriate page
& high lined in yellow
                    or blue or shocking pink. "Hi,"
he would say, my friend the high liner, "so what didja
see, anything good, anything sexy?" And I would say,
"O, The Bald Soprano, by Ionesco, it was really funny."
"O," he would say, "I saw that, they should do it in the
nude, make it more interesting." I collapse on an
available chair & pour out the beer I've brought upstairs.
"So what happens in Women in Love? How does the plot develop
to the point where Gerald loses his cool?" "O, I don't know,"
he'd say,
        "a couple of good parts, they fit right in to my
thesis," & he'd put his feet up on the desk & cover his short curly
red hair with both hands & moan like a goose.

You come in here with those bib overalls
& walk around
                    & I don't know what to do. You come in here
with those bib overalls with the carpenter's pencil
in the little ½ inch carpenter's pocket top left full breast
with no singlet or t-shirt.
                    It's summer, of course, it's hot,
& just a flash of pink tropical sherbet briefs
as you move your long arms
                    – there is a bib,
hence the name, but the overalls are cut low at each side
& loosely clipped with large steel buttons.
                    I don't know
if I should offer you a big double gin&tonic with lots of lime
or if I should excuse myself – another woman – & go for a walk
up to the store
                    or down to Bloor Street, look at some books,
a new biography of Georgia O'Keeffe, sounds interesting,
cappuccino at Prego Della Piazza,
                    or buy some ice cream.
It's hot,
        it's summer. I'm glad you live on my 3rd floor
walking barefoot on the polished hardwood of my living room
2nd floor & you've got a CD of Wallace Rooney
& ½ a fresh musk melon. I should listen,
                    but I don't want
last week to become a habit, I don't want to get involved,
that great gorgeous ball of yellow yarn my mother
used to roll across the living room. Moebius
                    is a beautiful

word,
       & I'm not exactly sure of what it means to people
in pure
mathematics. We come & go, it's traffic, I have no money,
I love the yellow Saab my neighbour across the street has bought
& parked in the apartment building drive
                             way. Life is perfect
in all its modular moments, I think Levi-Strauss invented
bib
overalls. We come & go, you make my mind the size of
the Pacific Ocean. I make you wet & then I enter you
& it is incorrect to say I make you come
                         but I seem
to. Night dark, you smell of fresh pine sawdust, sweat,
fresh laundry. I cook
            2 small salmon steaks for supper.

Wickson is a peculiar name – wick & son,
it's English & it's eccentric,
                            & plums are supposed to be natural
· & beautiful & part of God's effortless & eternal world,
so there,
Professor Wickson, California, the great state,
Stanford, I think,
                    bred this particular plum.
Bio-technology has been used for various useful things.
I have 4 of them sitting on my kitchen window sill
slowly ripening, showing slightly different patches of colour
from one day to the next.
                            The Ontario tomatoes are better,
vine-ripened field tomatoes.
I think the boys in physics should walk across the hall
& take over Bio-tech
                        & sort things out. Maybe they need
larger blackboards in Bio-tech, maybe they need a more macro
view of the universe & nature.
                                Clarence is here,
for supper & talk & drinks. I pick up 2 of the tomatoes
from the window sill & begin a simple salad of tomatoes
& green onions & parsley. Marion will be home around 6
& we'll talk about music. I sympathize entirely with Clarence,
he thinks the whole emphasis on poetry & art criticism
is sort of crazy, anything he can't play on an alto or a tenor,
although he likes novels & data screens,
Saxophone   really doesn't make a lot of sense. Lounges now
on the cane-back chair with his feet up over the table. Effortless,
like the beginning of a great solo as the different notes
build up to a statement of purpose.

They have been working since high school at a large chicken factory called Swift's. Moira is 17. She says that it's a big company, standing with her dress tucked into sloppy blue jeans, and rubber boots with the tops rolled down, not much point wearing running shoes, too much falling debris. "Not from plucking, stupid," Harriet said to one of the boys who took them for dinner at the Italian place over at Blenheim, "we don't pluck the fucken bastards, we tear them with our bare hands." She had held up one hand in the middle of eating her vitello picato or whatever the guy with the big moustache called it. "No we don't," Moira had said, she was in giggles, a big plastic bag of dark insanity, the 2 suits they were with were really getting their money's worth even though they weren't going to get laid, although Harriet thought her guy was sort of cute, he had a dark blue suit and short-cropped sandy hair and blue eyes. Sure, that's cute. The Co. isn't cute. The Co. just moves chickens on a conveyor belt. The girls tear them apart. The Co. makes money. They have been late about 5 times this month. Moira is chewing gum. Juicy Fruit. Harriet is chewing gum. Beeman's. You have to chew gum. It seems to keep the smell of fresh chicken and fresh chicken guts out of your nose. Harriet would rag her. She'd put on an accent like the Mayor's wife and she'd say, "No, I don't want those bloody chickens up my nasal passages." Moira would laugh despite herself. Harriet was the active one, Moira was the laugher, Moira could laugh at almost anything. "We should be communists," says Harriet, she's kidding. She always comes up with wild ideas, and then she breaks up and Moira breaks up too. Moira's standing there with a cigarette in her mouth. Not much raspberry lipstick left by 4:00 p.m. She's plump and giggles. Harriet's thin and dramatic with red hair. It's a big Co. Sure. Biggest except for the Rawlins Furniture Co. And you'll break your back in about 3 places for sure if you work over there. "They wouldn't know what to do with us then," she says. "They don't know what to do with us now," says Harriet. Moira brushes a stray bit of gizzard from the big white Co. apron you wear while you're working on the belt. It's stained like a county police accident blanket. "They'd piss themselves," she says. Her lips are a little tense. She thinks she's 6 weeks pregnant. Isn't totally sure for a fact. Doesn't know how the hell it happened. Tearing chickens apart since high school hasn't done her any harm. Just spoiled a few suppers and turned her off chickens. Must have made a mistake. "They'd barf their guts out, wouldn't they?" she says, letting her blue eyes run up and down the big wire-patterned frosted windows.

Momma, your boy has been drinking again
& is lost
          O yes, I am lost,
in the darkness of this world.
The fine yellow of the moon is strong, yes, that's true,
but great shifting mountains of darkness
swirl about like large waves of the sea. I suppose
you are going to say that if I didn't drink like this
I would be more successful. Okay. But it's a
foolish custom
that goes back to the 1950s & my father's time –
you remember him, Momma,
                              hopping on one leg
with his underwear around one ankle
& raising the bottle of Dewar's
up in his left hand in the middle of the kitchen;
not exactly *cucina futurisma*, I must admit,
like now, where I cook the fresh young tiger shrimp
in a little oil & balsamic vinegar
& serve them up with a sharp blueberry cassis
pointed with a few tspns of inexpensive
cognac,
          a province in France.
                              Well, maybe
you're ½ right, Momma, but
if I didn't drink like this
the darkness, my darkness which comes from my
childhood, would pile up like hidden storm
clouds
          & weigh me down. I know what you think.
You think I should meet someone just like you & then

I would not drink at all. But I would, sure.
Daddy did, living with you, right?
I would drink anyway.
And she would interfere & I would hate her.
I think my way is much better.
I work 50 hours a week,
I'm sleeping good & doing well. And I praise
god for making whiskey.
                    I don't think any woman
could allow me to relax & feel comfortable
the way that amber flow takes me with its quick heat
& lifts me up on the balls of my feet. Best chef
in Toronto, Momma. Best.
                    Nobody can touch my
crayfish, Momma. Nobody can touch my pork
loin with apricot slices & bits of pistachio nuts.

        Now it is dark & the magpies have gone to
sleep
     on the green lawns of the university in Capitol City,
Alberta, & I am ½ way through Idaho   going south
to a small town in Wyoming. Maybe
                    I'll stay in Laramie,
or maybe I'll move on, I don't know. The bus isn't all that
comfortable
        but I'm not sure what I'm looking for. Call it
something different from the East
& more exciting than Winnipeg photography exhibitions. The bus
rocks back & forth on the uneven road. It's about
2 in the morning, that's where the hands are
on my luminous watch. I slept after supper,
ham on dark bread, tomatoes, instead of
reading,
      or flirting with the girl across the aisle.
She's from Nebraska & was working in Calgary
as a waitress. There's a boyfriend in there somewhere
but I don't ask. "Strippers make more money," she says,
"but they're usually girls on drugs, & I sure don't
want anything like that." No, ma'am, not
               me. She thinks
my books, Baudrillard's inept *America*, & a novel called *Ransom*,
look interesting. I like to think about the history
of this route, but all I really want when I arrive in Laramie
is a different *kind* of main street. Sounds simple, doesn't it,
almost simple-minded? Okay, I'm working with simple forms.

Scott MacCloud on the cover of *NOW*, October 6, 1994. "Hey,"
says Dahlia
                tall & black & gorgeous
rolling a joint in the middle of the kitchen   where the copy of *NOW*
is lying on the kitchen table,
                                "What are these white boys into?"

"Search me," I say, "there are so many groups out there   all you
really need
                is not love   but simply an image, a Look
                                                like eyes
painted on a big Halloween pumpkin,
                                a gadget,
a gadget will do."
                        "Any gadget in a storm," says Alec,
he's sitting
over by the refrigerator finger drumming on the table
& there's a big blue jay
                        so help me God
sitting on an electric line outside the window. Alec's only criticism
is – none of these groups can play, they can't play a melodic line,

& they can't handle funky time signatures or 3-part chords.
                                                "So what
do they do?" says Dahlia holding up the sky blue joint. I say, "I don't
know, they've got a group called *Girls Against Boys*, and one of the guys
used to work in the same Washington, D.C., *pet store* as one of the guys
in that other Washington, D.C., group – *Fugazi.*"
                                "O," she says, "wow."

Tom Garrone, tall, curly dark hair, 26, was up in the blue air in the spring of 1986 in New York, tumbling, "Hey, what's going on? Hey, what's going on?" like a long arms, long-legged 6'3½" open-mouthed, tumbler pigeon.

And then he landed on his feet in May and it all began happening the way it was supposed to happen. 26 years old. Like natural.

Like natural, he lucked into a couple of trial songs, and then a whole album, post-punk dirges with some bright hopeful colour leaping up in the minimalist images – for a promising, going places group out of New Jersey originally called the Desperados.

Now he can pay the rent, and actually put money in the bank, and even more amazing – direct some of his attention back to his writing. Because what Tom really wants is to be a writer, and he wants to write a novel as good as *The Stranger* or as good as *100 Years of Solitude*.

Now the events in his life are happening much faster than they actually do in the lives of pigeons. They have already been down to Jackson, Miss., for a weekend gig, and gotten in trouble, and they played 3 places in Georgia, coming slowly back north, and one hot 2-night blitz at a club called HOT ZONE in Washington, D.C. They're back in New York now, with a large rented blue and white tour bus parked outside their rehearsal space warehouse, and Tom is already exhausted.

It's late afternoon and he's at a store on 34th Street called Madonna. He's buying a couple of shirts, one denim, and one white with vertical red and blue stripes, which seems like a fairly innocent thing to do on a late afternoon day. It's New York, there are millions of people, Tom isn't from New York, the weather outside is bucolic. And a song called "Girls Just Want to Have Fun" is going through his mind. Not for any special reason, it's catchy, it's a Cyndi Lauper song, he just likes the lead motif at the beginning of the song before her voice fades for a moment and the bass takes over.

Tonight there's a big send-off party for the Desperados before they take off tomorrow and the beginning of a midwestern tour, at least 4 or 5 weeks, he isn't really sure, a lot of hotels with sawdust on the floor, first stop – Bloomington, Ind. Bloomington, Ind., USA.

There's another album in the works, and he wants to work on it, and he wants to begin his novel about 2 musicians and a young woman botanist going to Florida to rediscover a friend's grandfather's farm. He likes this picture, and he likes his life in New York now that things have gotten better, now that he's not tumbling in the blue air. But he's not really crazy about the idea of going on this tour.

There won't be that much for him to do anyway, just hang out, do things with Whitney. Whitney is Tom's girlfriend, extraordinary, moody, beautiful, 24, ambivalent and quite often frustrating. Whitney is the sliding centre of Tom's mixed-up life these days. She's the fabulous young singer who fronts for the Desperados. She's a big fan of Tom's songs. But off-stage, unless they're in bed or having a late morning breakfast together, she tends to fluctuate all over New York.

So, he grabs a cab and heads downtown for 6th Street.

Tom arrives at the party around 8 o'clock. Loaded with parcels, he didn't want to bother going home first, he was coming south by cab anyway. The party started early, it's been going for hours, some of the guys are planning to knock off early around 12, Hayden, the arranger and keyboard player, is expecting some magazine people.

The huge main room of the loft is full of people, painters, photographers, musicians from other groups, friends, and ex-wives.

He spots Jack from a distance. Jack said he'd meet him here, and Tom didn't stop for supper on his way south anyway, he just stopped for a hot veal sandwich and some coffee. He waves, he can talk to Jack later. Whitney is here, although where Tom isn't sure and doesn't stop to think especially, Whitney can take care of herself. He puts the parcels at the far end of the improvised bar, gets a drink, a nice cold Lite beer, and sure, ok, he'll try one Fletcher's, a notorious southern whiskey of about 86 proof. Then he surveys the crowd.

Whitney is wandering around, several blocks away at the far end of the enormous room. There are lots of people, wall to wall, as the saying goes, if you're into walls. Not really Tom's best atmosphere. Tom is conscious of

Whitney wandering loose like the mythological fox his father used to tell him about who set the corn fields on fire. Maybe the fields in the story were wheat fields, Tom can't remember all the details from his father's stories.

"Whitney," he said to her, sitting in the Blue Gulf Donut Shop in Jackson, Miss., "this is all going to work. My songs, your voice, you're great on stage, and you've got Susan Sarandon legs from here to Wichita."

A slight frown of concern had waltzed across her oval elegant face, sitting there in the Blue Gulf. "What I don't like," she said, and her voice was slower but more Vassar/California than usual, despite the Hawaiian tokes they had done up and away in the parking lot, Tom sprawled on the front seat, bliss, with his head in Whitney's lap and one foot out the window, after the concert. "What I don't like is the way that everything shifts sometimes after I sing; and the fans are applauding, and I think I've done something really brilliant, all the attention suddenly shifts to somebody like Mason talking about the goddamn governor of Mississippi. I don't like it," she said, "it's not that I disagree with what they're saying. Fuck," she said, enjoying the word, "I'm not a smooth supperclub fox, or whatever that southerner Mason may think. But Tom, I am a lady. I'm a singer. And I think they should fucking well respect that, don't you, Tom, think they should respect me?" It was warm, it was night, and she was troubled.

Of course he had said yes. He loves Whitney's voice. It sends shivers of fine blue ice and raw bird bone up and down his long back. But sometimes he isn't sure if she sees the Desperados as a complete band, or does she see it as a black-white blues band that she gets in front of and tears up brilliant caricatures of Helen Morgan?

Tom has a dry mouth and a visible blue vein under one huge grey eye, but the tall guy is cracking gum over the heads of about 150 friends of the Desperados in a new white cotton jacket lapels, you know, the works, big flap painter's pockets and a bright red green & yellow Hawaiian shirt that signals every movement.

Most but not all of the 150 people in this loft are under 30, but there is lots of diversity. There are photographers, a few painters, they're not all music people.

Odd things happen. New York is full of illusions. Surprises abound in every loft or bar of the city. This tall blonde girl walking past Tom is naked from the bright sash waist of her faded blue denims. She has a lovely enigmatic blue-eyed smile and she has nothing but shaving cream, or maybe shampoo, thick white open swirls, on her full perfect but rather arrogant white breasts.

Tomorrow they leave on their western tour. To take America by storm, the America outside of New York & New Jersey, that is. This is not the night to think about abstractions like permanence, or the epistemology of purpose, or what is the true nature of true love. Ideas like that are as boring and heavy as empty biscuit boxes weighted with leadfoil. This is a good night to get drunk, to see how much it is possible for you to drink in one single sustained unbroken rush in one evening, to get laid, to make love with your honey or with someone else's main squeeze or eternal delight, to Turkish the harem, or to Harem the turks, slap your best friends on the back repeatedly, hang out the big 1890s industrial windows looking down on East 6th; drop down paper bags of water on other friends' heads, whatever.

It's crowded, warm and a little smoky despite the open windows. Jack appears from behind several couples and a bass saxophone, he's wearing a dark blue blazer, double-breasted, and chinos, he looks academic and confused. He gives Tom a hug and says something about rock & roll, and Tom gestures with a wide abrasive hand. "How am I supposed to keep my mind on writing great songs when there are beautiful people walking around taking their clothes off?" He's conscious of his voice saying people, rather than girls, for example, gender conscious, all the Desperados tend to be politically correct even down to what magazines they read. *Rolling Stone* is good, *New York Magazine* is shit. And also of the crowds, the warmth, and of being a little drunk although it's still fairly early evening. He's also conscious of being rather proud of the party to which he's invited Jack, the number of interesting people, this ridiculously beautiful girl, the music, Tom feels he's way up in the world, above the net baskets, walking on clouds.

"You're just hard luck," says Jack, "it's because you're a bull-headed Italian guy, and you don't subscribe to *Paris Review*.

Tom shrugs off the sensitive *Paris Review* comment and says that he thinks the girl is at least as beautiful as Botticelli's Venus coming out of the sea. He should know, shouldn't he? Tom says he wouldn't want, he means desire, the girl himself. But that she would be wonderful for Henry.

Henry is an ex teaching assistant in philosophy at NYU, and a friend of Jack and Tom's. He's a short, rumpled 2nd generation Czechoslovakian guy about 35, and he now works as a book-store clerk down west of the village. Jack used to work with Henry at one point before he got this cushy new job in a feed warehouse as an inventory clerk which allows him to read magazines all day and still dream, to some degree, of becoming a writer. Tom used to go to films with Henry a lot in the afternoons, European films. Tom was the expert on Italian, Rossellini, for example, and Henry was the expert on East European, Skolimowicz, Wajda, people of that approach.

The girl's breasts are rather wonderful, they make him think of a Man Ray poster he's seen, full, uplifted, the rosy nipples poke through the white shaving cream like plump rosebuds. Too good for Henry, his friend, the expert on Hegel, the expert on Strauss, who is at this moment as far as Tom knows somewhere out by the kitchen where there is more food than an army of tartar press agents could eat. Henry, although short, caustic, and not very heavy, is quite a gourmet, or gourmand, one of the two.

A kid with blond hair and dark blue shades leans over Vitalis and dabs a touch of cream off with his forefinger, tastes it and makes an enormous face. "I thought it was whipping cream," he says outraged. The girl smiles irresponsibly, in love with herself as a phenomenon. She probably has a Ph.D.

Just a joke, more beautiful than guys mooning out of '67 Buicks, he guesses, tongue in his mouth. He tries to remain cool. This is part of his new role in life apparently, to be less animated more clean-shaven, cooler, more a making the scene kind of guy whereas before he was the quintessence of the casual but animated, all out on the surface emotions pinned to his torn sleeve waiting for the vultures to get at him, to hit on him.

The girl passes she's almost up to his chin long legs tight black leather boots swinging one perfect hip exaggeratedly to get around a craggy hulk of a guy, a producer someone said innocently, with a full reddish beard and stained brown leather western hat on the other side of Tom. His left eye flops like a heron plunging after fish some early dawn childhood morning on eastern Lake Erie. Even calmed down by the Gallo, he's been drinking plastic glassfuls, Tom's not too cool. He's usually a fairly laconic guy, but these band events and his new-found prestige make him a little dizzy and excited, put him in a sort of overdrive, make him a bit of a show-off.

Whitney is part of this problem. He has no sooner lucked in, if indeed it is luck, to becoming a songwriter and receiving one of his first big cheques, than suddenly Whitney is singing for the group and getting all kinds of attention.

Jack speaks light-heartedly to her, the dog, well, he leans forward politely, smiling that earnest graduate school steel-rims smile, and says, "Do you want my jacket? There's a handkerchief in the pocket you can use."

The tall beautiful girl gives Jack a smile full of warm irony and bats blue eyes like cool banjos. "No, it's okay," she says in a clear Boston voice, "I'm just doing this to advertise a friend's album. Besides," she adds, "I'm afraid we might get a lot of this Gillette shaving cream all over your jacket." Tom watches her disappear lazily into the crowd of people like a jogger disappearing into a subway crowd.

"You didn't tell me she was a friend of yours," he says to Jack with mock dumb resentment.

"Just an acquaintance." Jack looks embarrassed. He was meant to be a Fine Arts instructor. That was years ago, already time seems like a fluid, elliptical elastic band. Jack is 27 now. Jack started writing during his last undergraduate year in Kansas. Then he changed to English. Then he dropped out and came to New York and met Tom.

"There are millions of girls here," Tom says, "and they've all got that 'it' look."

Jack laughs. "You've got gorgeous Whitney. How do you find the time to be interested?"

"Not me, fella, I'm taken." He is indeed, or he would like to be.

But actually Whitney is beautiful and a constant headache.

"Okay," says Jack, "look, we'll make it a project, it'll be fun, like the time we did the green hornet postering campaign all over West 29th. We'll get Henry laid. Henry's terrific but he doesn't make enough moves. With the wildest girl here. Just like in one of those cornball French comedies, you know, angst and humour. It'll be fun. It won't be hard. Let's do it."

Tom doesn't think this sounds very much like García Márquez and Albert Camus talking about the soul of humanity; but of course, these 2 completely separate, different periods as the academics say, heroes of Tom's lambent literary side, never did have a chance to meet.

Whitney is on the other side of the room jawing with a smooth-shaven Aramis type guy from some publication like *Vanity Fair*. He was introduced to the guy, who has a handshake like a large pink and white clam, and the guy made a big production out of the fact that he used to be a fashion asst. for Conde Nast. Maybe they're talking about fashion. Whitney loves fashion. Whitney looks delicious. She looks especially delicious tonight. She spent the night with Tom, but she doesn't look tired. Women are different, Tom thinks, they don't get tired, they just get up the next morning and shower. The more sex they get the more energy they seem to have. Whitney is fresh and vivacious, her hands moving in huge blue and gold circles, busy plugging the new Desperados LP with considerable verve. No expenditure of sperm. Women just become more and more energetic. Tom reflects vaguely at times on the feasibility of practising carezza. The Turks may have something.

Jack and Tom used to have good discussions about sex, they weren't discussions so much as they were conversations, exchanges. Jack would tell Tom about some escapade and Tom would supply comments appreciative or sympathetic and then Tom would tell Jack about some escapade. Their conversations weren't locker-room style, and apart from the fact that they're both guys and fairly tall guys, their conversations could easily be said to have a similarity to girl-talk.

This changed of course after Jack got married and had a child. Now Jack is very simplistic on the subject. He likes his domestic situation, complains about money sometimes, not having enough time to write, and tells Tom stories about how smart his daughter is, she's 2½, cute, and smart as a whip.

Tom would like a permanent relationship, but he's only 26 and looking vaguely ahead at the rosy abyss of 30. He likes hanging out with the group, and being able to move freely from one place to another in the evening, the line-ups are too big at Max's Kansas City, he goes to hear blues groups at the Trading Company, and often wanders from there to Phil's Bar or the Mohican Diner with its large orange and blue neon Indian head facing north up Lexington. He reads a lot, Albert Camus and books about Camus's Algeria, and of course he has read all the novels and stories of Paul Bowles, liking *The Sheltering Sky* about the best.

Tom does 50 push-ups every morning, makes a ritual, despite the dilapidated bathroom, of turning up the shower to almost scalding and then reversing it to ice-cold for a minute or two. He diets despite the fact that he doesn't need to: it isn't hard on Tom's budget; tortellini soup, chicken gumbo or soup with an egg. Morning hard-ons are part of this exercise: first thing in the morning Tom will leap out of bed, if he's alone, that is, and hang shirts, sweaters, even a jacket sometimes on the levitating member, the white Tuscan eel that wants to be airborne. These simple, childish perhaps, games convince Tom of 2 things: 1, he is still young; 2, he will never die.

Over beer one night at Chuga's, they were both a little drunk, Jack leaned over and put his hands on Tom's shoulders, with affection, nothing smart alec, big smile on his face, and said, "You know, I really love you, Tom. I think you're fucken queer." It was meant with affection; it was, in a sense, a comment on Jack's marriage. Jack is on the verge of giving up his warehouse job, which Tom thinks is a good job for him, and of becoming an office worker. This in Tom's eyes would make his best friend one of the fallen.

Not having played basketball for over 6 years, Tom is obsessive about the Calvin Klein underwear ads. He wants his own body to be at least that good and doesn't want it to change, ever.

Bitterly discouraged in a long love affair with an older woman in 4th year he feels, although very casual on the surface, that there is no reason why men shouldn't be as least as attractive to women as women are to men, if not more. Tom has an ego. One mouth, 2 eyes, 2 nipples, 2 hands and a big ego.

"Those nomads," Jack tells him one afternoon, "as far as I know those guys don't smoke cigarettes, Tom."

He gives up Gauloises, which is what Camus smoked; he smokes Camels now, he loves the picture of the camel on the front of the package. Also, they taste better. And they're cheap.

A somewhat more relaxed and slightly juiced Tom Garrone, 26, songwriter, and Mason, the devastating young bassist from the Desperados, who came up with the perfect bass chords for the bridge in the middle of Tom's recent hit single about a laid-off worker leaving a small town in Mississippi and moving to Texas, and a small crowd of other people are hanging out in front of the 4th floor john.

A young woman who looks like Katharine Ross, but artsy and she's got red hair, well-dressed, casual black linen open-necked suit, stands out in the group. For more reasons than General Motors has excuses. She has great legs, she's wearing heels, fabulous aqua-marine eyes, plus she has a large pure white silky borzoi dog, on a leash.

The warehouse john had broken down around 7 o'clock for some reason and Hayden, tall, sardonic, affable, dark pigmentation American, also the composer for the group, since he was in the area, commandeered the telephone and got in touch with a Spanish guy over on 7th who could apparently fix anything with threads at either end.

"You look after this lady's dog," Hayden tells him. "I've got to go and get myself a cold beer and talk to Bats." Bats Ekberg is the drummer for the Desperados; like Tom, he's originally from Toronto.

Tom smiles at her. "You seem to be at the head of the line," he says.

"I think I'm first, I've been here for hours," says a plump girl with steel rims and a shaven head with neat little cross-lines running back and forth across her head like drunken Xs & Os. Sort of a grid haircut, suggesting some sort of affinity with gridlock, street maps, office floor designs, urban planning, UFOs, or radar screens.

"You have indeed," says Red very graciously. She brushes an imaginary white Borzoi from her gorgeous unbuttoned suit.

The young woman fiddler across the room, 75% obscured by moving blurs of multicoloured people, is leaning with her back against one of the large industrial windows. She's not participating in conversation very much with Whitney any more. Whitney is talking with her hands now, quite enthusiastic about something. The guy called Henner, important enough, well, he's the group's manager, older guy, suit; stupid name, Tom can't quite see his face, just a corner of it from where he is standing, but the guy is obviously pitching something with a bit of a slant to Whitney. He looks a bit like a much older cousin. Sort of an interesting face, but weathered, slightly distorted. Tom has an odd flash of a Korean War veteran's face, but very brief, fleeting, wonders about him.

Mason licks a flake of Durham from his lip and nods as he picks up on Tom's attention.

"I really like your dog. He looks athletic," Tom says to the girl.

"My name's Laura," she says, "Laura Redfield." She holds out a calm gloved hand.

"Tom Garrone. I'm the songwriter." He feels proud. The subtle shaded V at the top of her top button, she has no blouse underneath, is beginning to excite him.

Tom gets excited easily, but it's mostly walking on fences. People are very loose about sex in the group. They're hard on drugs but they're pretty loose on sex. He feels he should try out a few numbers, but doesn't know himself how serious he is.

"I'm a graphic artist," she says, "actually, right now at least, I do a lot of photo research. Weird things." She gestures airily, mock airily. "UFOs for a magazine article. Southern poor families who live on tinned possum meat." She laughs, she thinks this last remark is apparently funny, almost daintily at first, and then breaks up; when she breaks up laughing she strikes Tom as extremely sexy, he wants to get into bed with her right this minute, what the hell, maybe the washroom, at least it's got a door. He's slightly drunk.

He should probably go back to nothing but Lite beer. Meanwhile of course he's still watching Whitney. This whole business of being so stacked on Whitney, and, at the same time, there being always so many other people around is beginning to faze and fumble on him. His big head is beginning to slip. It makes him a little dizzy.

"Woops," she says gustily as the plump girl comes out of the john and a young guy with romantic chestnut brown hair down past his shoulders, 60s revival neo 60s Sassoon, not hip at all, is about, glancing at Laura as he does so, to Gabriel into the can.

She puts one gloved hand gently on Sassoon's shoulder. "Do pardon me," she says to the Gabriel look-alike, "I simply must pee. Otherwise," she grins at Tom, whom she obviously likes but it's all so crazy, what does it all mean, people floating about glancing off each other like atoms bombarding the inside of an accelerator, "my dog will get upset."

She leaves Borzoi to guard the door and sails in smoothing her skirt very deliberately across her buttocks for no apparent reason other than flair or flirtation.

"Mason," says Tom to Mason, sounding more like Mason than like himself, "my nostrils are full of Opium by St. Laurent."

"Easy boy," Mason has a long draw on his handrolled cigarette and grins philosophically at Tom, almost squinting, "you've got to loosen up a little. You've got the star over there. What's your problem? You heard what Hayden said," he adds, "you've got to open up the bass notes on those songs. Got to cool down. We're pulling out tomorrow. Tour bus galore. This is a big tour," he says, "you've got to walk easy unless you're busy on stage."

Tom imagines he can hear the sound of the beautiful red-haired girl's golden urine tinkling against the dusty white porcelain toilet bowl over and above the multiple sounds of the revelry.

Although last night with Whitney more than satisfied Tom's basic carnal drives and animal needs, he's wired for erotic signals, maybe as a result of living a quiet life on small dollars per week at the 12x16 container on East 16th, and seeing Barbara, wonderful but not bizazzy, 4 or 5 times a week. Whatever the causality, metaphysics doesn't really have to come into it. Tom was a little on the shy side in late high school, or so he remembers, but has been somewhat wired fritzed shunted for erotic pulselights since sometime after college.

The girl's perfume, red hair, she said her name was Laura, lingers in the air as he stands leaning against the wall outside the loft washroom talking to Mason. Tom is a little drunk, that's one thing, well, almost drunk, one big double belt of Scotch that Yvonne gave him from a fifth in her handbag, "You'll like this," she said, "this is what you guys drink up north isn't it?" and 4 or 5 Gallos have certainly made him a little loose. And parties seem to affect him this way, they rub him one way, he feels smothered, who are all these people, he'd like to be back in his favourite bar talking to his friend Jack, who is here somewhere now, or he'd like to be back in the Widener Library at Harvard, reading some of the material on the first Italian writers in New York, in the 1920s; but parties also affect him in the second way, they rev him, stoke him, shake him around, make him feel like doing various odd crazy manic things.

So here he is, it's a bit late in the evening, it's getting dark outside, this party is probably going to go until the small hours although the Desperados themselves have to get up fairly early in the morning and pull out for Chicago (but that won't stop them from partying all night if they feel like it, the crazy guys); and Tom is leaning against the wall talking to Mason who is actually talking to somebody else and Tom has all sorts of pretty colours going through his big head: party colours, sounds, the girl with red hair, that's how he thinks of her, Laura. He leans down and pats the dog's head, Borzoi, is that his name? The dog slants his head to the side and looks at him quizzically. Blue eyes, Tom thinks, since when do dogs have blue eyes?

When Laura comes out, surrendering the washroom to Sassoon, Tom leans against the wall and talks to her very intimately. "I think we should probably get together," he says, "have lunch," forgetting that he and the Desperados, and Whitney, whom he seems to have forgotten about for the moment, are all going to be packing up and out of town by tomorrow afternoon, "someplace outdoors and sunny. I think we both have a lot to talk about."

"And what about Borzoi?" she says. "I never have lunch without him."

She smooths her thick glossy red hair back with one hand, thrusting her upper body forward slightly. Tom takes this in. Her hips swivel a titch. Tom reacts. He puts one hand on her shoulder.

"I think you're really lovely," he says, "marry me." The dog growls. It's a very soft low sibilant growl, not what you would normally think of as a dog growl at all.

"O not yet," she says perkily, "shouldn't we have some sort of courtship, go to Hawaii for a couple of weeks first or something like that? This guy over at the Buster Keaton Advertising Co. on 57th asked me if I'd like to go to Bermuda to go marlin fishing a couple of weeks ago. And I said, Marlin fishing? I don't even know how to fish for trout. My father goes fishing," she says sadly, as if this fact is a momentary blister on the otherwise perfect face of reality. She has a very fine line of light brown freckles across the bridge of her nose. Tom has a momentary semi, just a shift of emphasis, a faint bulge, nothing serious as yet. Besides he has loose pants on, must stop wearing jeans, no one else does any more, and the loose white jacket with the flap pockets is quite concealing, discreet.

He puts a hand on each of her trim black linen shoulders and kisses her, quite a long kiss, right there in front of everybody outside the washroom door. Hey, marry her, fella, somebody anonymous calls from out of the crowd.

She kisses back, this is true, mouth slightly parted, hips loose, hands half-raised, but doesn't open her mouth, doesn't put her tongue, no, that would be a bit much, in his handsome mouth.

Borzoi rises to the occasion and jumps up with his feathery white front paws on their shoulders, as if either trying to separate them or perhaps enter their embrace. Tom's hand brushes her breast as they disengage. She kisses his hand.

Tom is not totally unaware of most of the party, exactly where they are, has forgotten about Whitney, who is obviously here somewhere, and has totally forgotten about the fact that they are going out of town tomorrow.

"It's really hot in here," says Tom uncomfortably, a little flushed, "why don't we get some fresh air and a cool drink down the street?" He doesn't know exactly where they should go, he simply has the automatic impulse that he would like the two of them, uh uh, 3, counting Borzoi, to get out to the freedom of the street. Freedom of the street, he thinks to himself, clichés, this is a cliché and I'm acting it out.

"I'll be a second," she says, "don't go away, just wait here and I'll be right back. Riiight back," she adds. Borzoi trots dutifully behind Red's gorgeous derrière as she sashays through crowds of people in the general direction of the improvised long table and planks and packing cases bar.

Of course she never comes back, and by the time that Tom realizes she was probably on her way home for the evening when she stopped for a quick pee in the first place, several other things have changed. He is a little soberer, a little dulled, and he has a small fierce little triphammer of a headache starting up somewhere in the far left side of his head.

He sees Mason standing a few feet away, leaning against the rough plaster wall and hopes he doesn't look foolish.

"You are completely right, Mase," he says. He slaps Mason on the shoulder. "Ok," he says, "I think I've had too much to drink. I'm gonna get some air."

"You've got to drink Lightning more slowly," says Mason, as Tom ambles, turning this way and that, across the room to where Whitney is talking to Henner.

But when he arrives at the far west side of the room, he finds, by the big industrial window, the fiddler woman with a bright Peruvian vest, talking to a couple of girlfriends about how great Maria Muldaur is, and how stupid men are about cooking. "I mean," she says, "they're so beautiful, and you really try to love them in the best way you can; but, fuck, they don't even wash up the pots, not even the pots, after they do simple things like steak and mashed potatoes."

"I never eat beef," one of her friends says, "chicken, I eat chicken once or twice a week. I don't even like to see a chicken get killed."

"Ok, then, chicken. They don't even wash up the pots afterwards after they've done some chicken." She turns to Tom. "You're looking for somebody," she says.

"Yeah, uh, tall slim dark girl, bright lipstick, sort of classy looking. She was standing right here talking to some old guy."

"Some old guy?" the country rock fiddler says. "You mean hen-killer Henner? That hawk-eyed fart. Grover, my boyfriend, was in a group he managed. I think they split." She says this with a gesture of vague hopefulness.

"Split?"

"I don't know. I think they were heading for the front door."

So, Whitney has done one of her famous splits, this time with the vaguely degenerate manager of the group, an older guy, a coke user, and a guy Tom doesn't particularly like, in contrast to the healthy 20somethings radical character of the Desperados themselves. Hayden is involved in some business deal on a different floor. Laura has apparently split also, with her impressive dog. And Tom himself feels strangely satisfied and also hungry. It's about 10:30 or somewhere around there, the band is heading for Bloomington, Ind., and the Desperados' farewell is beginning, for Tom, to collapse around his large handsome head like a crayon-coloured brown paper bag.

He hears the women's laughter over his shoulder as he wanders through the group of people in the direction of the kitchen.

The scene in the kitchen, not a small room by any means, is not bizarre or spectacular, but, nevertheless, it knocks Tom for a loop.

The grey & orange tiled counter space around the double sink at the far wall has been supplanted by a long trestle table set up to accommodate a variety of plates and bowls eventually bound for the main room and hungry people's happy mouths. A large plump French guy with marcelled blond hair in a tall floppy white chef's hat and big over-size white apron is doing up 2 large frying pans of veal meatballs. An asst. sans floppy whites is washing mussels, or clams maybe, over by the sink. This is fragrant.

"Are the clams good?" he asks a young outofwork answer to Peter Townshend.

"Mussels. Fabulous," he says, "they're out of this world."

He walks over to the main counter and gets a plate with a green stripe from one of 2 stacks that are sitting there. A guy with a pony tail, these guys must be ex sailors or navigators of something, gestures at a pile of clean forks & knives and Tom gets a helping of fresh mussels from the big cook

Marcel. The mussels look nice and fat inside the black crusty shells with little bits of onion, black olives and pimento and lots of red juice steaming up from the plate.

He leans against the wall with the noises of the stove behind him and somebody's bass starting up in the next room (several groups are sitting in fooling around blues mostly to provide some live music for the send off) and he eats about ½ the plate of mussels slowly and feels refreshed.

Wiping his mouth with a folded napkin from a stack by the side of one of the small ovens Tom looks up surprised and sees Laura standing in the kitchen doorway with a drink in her hand. He wonders vaguely if it's the same drink, probably yes, perhaps not. She smiles as if with a great satisfaction, as if she has just accomplished some mission or endeavour of some kind. The dog is still with her, looking inquisitively at one of the tables on which presumably there is something that smells good.

"Come on in," he says, "the water's wonderful." He wonders what the dog does all day when she goes to work, he has an image of her in the morning shower, caps of white soap tumbling from her bright red hair, her breasts. Then he wonders if perhaps some agency or person has actually sent her to New York.

"Hmmm, no," she puts one hand on her trim stomach and shakes her head deliciously, "I couldn't eat a thing. I'll feel hungry later on. You've eaten."

"Ah, sure, why? Do I have a food stain on my new shirt?" He's wearing a pale blue denim shirt.

"No," she says, "it looks great." When she says this and puts her hand against his chest he takes her in his arms and kisses her.

In the big yellow cab heading west on 59th to where she lives, somewhere around Columbus Circle, she leans back in the seat and puts her head on his shoulder. "I'm exhausted," she says. The driver is fumbling around with the car radio and tunes in on an old 1977 song by Meat Loaf called "Paradise by the Dashboard Light." Tom remembers the song, he feels almost nostalgic, he was still in college.

"Do you remember this song, 'Paradise on the Dashboard'?" he asks her, misremembering the title, letting one casual hand flop on her white knee, in the dark of the cab her knee has an almost bright glowing colour.

"No," she says mysteriously, "I was in the southwest . . ."

"Oh," he says. The dog sits in the front seat head sometimes weaving from side to side, mouth open, panting.

ACKNOWLEDGEMENTS

Some of these works have appeared in same or different versions in the following magazines and imprints: *Canadian Fiction Magazine*, 20th Anniversary Issue; *Descant*; *Exile*; *This Magazine*; *Quarry*; and a special limited edition chapbook by "L e t t e r s book shop," prop. Nicky Drombolis. The author would like to take the occasion to thank these editors and various people like Peter McPhee, Ayanna Black, Gord Robertson, Lelah Ferguson, who have made intelligent suggestions, as well as Stan Dragland and the editorial department at McClelland & Stewart.

The author would also like to thank the Canada Council, the Ontario Arts Council, and the Toronto Arts Council for their support.